*Golf in Eastern Wisconsin*

*"This book is a great resource for enjoying some of the best public courses in the world, and they're right here in my home state of Wisconsin."*
**- Steve Stricker, PGA Tour star**

# Golf in Eastern Wisconsin
*A Destination Golf Course Guide*

© 2015 Michael J. Dauplaise

First Edition
All Rights Reserved. The author grants no assignable permission to reproduce for resale or redistribution. This license is limited to the individual purchaser and does not extend to others. Permission to reproduce these materials for any other purpose must be obtained in writing from the publisher except for the use of brief quotations within book chapters.

**Disclaimer**
Because of the dynamic nature of the Internet, any web addresses contained in this book may have changed since publication and may no longer be valid. In addition, all course descriptions were accurate as of the publication date. The views expressed in this work are solely those of the author and do not necessarily reflect the views of the publisher, and the publisher hereby disclaims any responsibility for them. In the event you use any of the information in this book for yourself, which is your constitutional right, the author and the publisher assume no responsibility for your actions.

Front cover photo of Whistling Straits courtesy Kohler Co.
Back cover photo of Erin Hills by the author

ISBN 10: 1942731132
ISBN 13: 978-1-942731-13-9

Published by M&B Global Solutions Inc.
United States of America (USA)

# Golf in Eastern Wisconsin

*A Destination Golf Course Guide*

**Mike Dauplaise**

*Golf in Eastern Wisconsin*

# **Dedication**

To my awesome wife and partner through all things that life brings. Although Bonnie is not a golfer, she encourages me to get out and play because she knows it's good for my mental health and I truly enjoy it. Thanks, babe. I love you!

*Golf in Eastern Wisconsin*

# Contents

| | |
|---|---|
| Foreword | 9 |
| Introduction | 13 |
| The Kohler Story | 15 |
| Whistling Straits | 19 |
| The Irish Course | 35 |
| The River Course | 49 |
| The Meadow Valleys Course | 65 |
| The Bull at Pinehurst Farms | 79 |
| Erin Hills | 97 |
| The Bog | 113 |
| Brown County | 127 |
| Acknowledgements | 143 |
| About the Author | 145 |

*Golf in Eastern Wisconsin*

# Foreword

## *By Pete Dye*

When Herb Kohler first approached me in 1984 about designing a championship golf course on land the Kohler Company owned in Eastern Wisconsin, I never would have guessed the project would evolve over the years into one of the top golf destinations in the world. The village of Kohler (pop. 2,000) was not exactly the center of the golfing universe.

I really underestimated the passion of Mr. Kohler and the pent-up enthusiasm that players in the region have for high-level golf. While Wisconsin features many quality public golf courses, very few at the time rose to the level of elite status. With only a six-month playing season most years, it was difficult to imagine how such an investment would pay dividends.

However, Mr. Kohler was insistent that golf would be the perfect complement to the American Club, the luxury spa and resort that adorns the main street in Kohler. The American Club is the only AAA Five Diamond Resort hotel in the Midwest, and Mr. Kohler was convinced that championship-caliber golf would draw additional guests and appeal to the hotel's clientele.

Mr. Kohler showed me some beautiful acreage not far from the Kohler factory that previously had been used for hunting. From a golf course designer's perspective, the property offered a variety of natural features ideal for designing a challenging layout. The Sheboygan River wound its way through the grounds, along with a number of feeder streams, rolling hills and wooded areas. Better yet, Mr. Kohler gave me free reign to use whatever portion of the property I wished.

I was only a few years removed from the debut of The Players Course, Ponte Vedra, Florida, which had received a great deal of attention for its radical design at the time. Mr. Kohler wanted Blackwolf Run to blend more with the natural terrain than the Players Course, yet retain some of the memorable qualities that would draw players from around the world.

Construction took place over the course of two short Wisconsin summers. As we were nearing completion in the late summer of 1986, a horrendous storm hit the area, dumping eight inches of rain in just four hours. The rushing water destroyed most of what we had worked so hard to create. It was absolutely heartbreaking. However, Mr. Kohler greeted me and the crew with a simple question, "When do you fellows plan to start back to work?" We got back restoring the course that day.

The storm added an extra year to the project, but when Blackwolf Run finally opened for play in 1988, the response was beyond positive. These enthusiastic Wisconsin golfers, who will play in almost any weather condition, filled the tee sheet and waited in lines outside the pro shop to play Mr. Kohler's pride and joy. It didn't take long for Mr. Kohler to call me with the order, "We need another eighteen holes."

Because of the original course's location in relation to the clubhouse and the Sheboygan River, I needed to route the next eighteen holes on the back sides of the original nines. This split the Blackwolf Run property into the River Course and the Meadow Valleys Course. However, the United States Golf Association still used the original course for the two U.S. Women's Open championships it has hosted there so far.

The unquestioned success of the Blackwolf Run courses predictably had Mr. Kohler thinking even bigger for his next project. This time, he presented me with relatively nondescript property along Lake Michigan about nine miles northeast of Kohler. Mr. Kohler's charge for Alice and me was to create a seaside American links course that would look like Ballybunion in Ireland.

Unlike the rolling, treed property I had to work with at Blackwolf Run, the property for creating Whistling Straits was like starting with a blank canvas. A former airstrip had left the acreage empty of any desirable features, so we would have to create the topography that would become the golf course.

Whistling Straits quickly garnered international attention; so much so that the PGA of America already targeted the course to host the 2004 PGA Championship prior to its opening in 1998. This unique golf attraction would go on to host other major championships, and in 2020 it will host perhaps the ultimate prize in the Ryder Cup Matches.

The Irish Course, which sits just inland next to the Straits Course, opened two years later. While it may not receive the attention of its big brother, the Irish Course stands on its own in terms of quality of design and shot-making requirements.

As of this writing, Mr. Kohler is in the early stages of planning a fifth golf course just south of the city of Sheboygan. As I think back thirty years, I never could have imagined the journey that would result from those first conversations. I am proud to have played a role in bringing his ever-expanding vision to reality and making this little corner of Wisconsin one of the world's great golf destinations.

*Pete Dye*

*Golf in Eastern Wisconsin*

# Introduction

As someone who has enjoyed his share of golf destination trips, I'm used to dealing with travel and lodging challenges when putting together a fun experience. Sometimes, however, it's easy to overlook destinations right under our nose.

That was the case for me while strategizing regions around the United States that might make for a good golf destination book. Eastern Wisconsin is my backyard. I live in Green Bay, which is only an hour north of Kohler, the center of the golf universe in this part of the world. Like the great venue we Packers fans have at our disposal to watch our favorite professional football team in Lambeau Field, locals sometimes take for granted what others consider a bucket list destination.

The golf courses featured in this book are worthy of a special trip in their own right, but viewed collectively, they stand above most as one of the great golf destinations in the country, if not the world. According to the 2015 *Golf Digest* rankings, Wisconsin is one of only two states in the country that can boast two top-ten courses on the magazine's list of America's 100 Greatest Public Courses (Oregon being the other). Would you have guessed that? I live here, and I didn't know it.

The site of major championships for the PGA, LPGA and Champions tours, a United States Amateur, and the 2020 Ryder Cup matches, Eastern Wisconsin offers a variety of public-access excellence that draws players of all levels from all over the world. The courses range from world famous to regionally well known, and all of them offer golf experiences worthy of a special visit. Some make a little bigger dent in the wallet than others, but you can expect that when dealing with elite properties.

Interestingly, one course in particular (Erin Hills) is a top-ten course which has not gained the level of name recognition even within Wisconsin that you would expect. This is changing quickly thanks to that venue's hosting the 2017 U.S. Open, the first ever contested in Wisconsin.

The four seasons we enjoy in Wisconsin make it impossible to play golf year round. Maybe that's why we're fanatical about playing as often as possible when conditions are favorable.

We're proud to call these fantastic golf courses our own and that all are open to the public. Pack your clubs and come for a visit. You just might be surprised at the quality of golf here in the Badger State.

Mike Dauplaise
May 2015

# The Kohler Story

Herbert V. Kohler Jr. barely knew the first thing about golf when guests at the Kohler Company's new American Club began stuffing the suggestion box with requests for a golf venue worthy of the world-class resort hotel.

Little did the company's long-time chief executive officer and president realize, but this gentle prodding from his guests was about to send him and his family's venerable company toward a business expansion that eventually would rank him among the most influential and important people in all of golf.

The Kohler Company, long an industry leader in kitchen and bath products, quickly became a world leader in the hospitality and golf businesses thanks to Mr. Kohler's foresight and willingness to invest in the little Wisconsin village founded by his grandfather.

Austrian immigrant John Michael Kohler was twenty-nine years old in 1873 when he purchased a majority interest in an iron foundry and machine shop in the lakeshore community of Sheboygan from his new father-in-law. That $5,000 investment gained him entry into the business of making machinery and farm implements. But it wasn't until ten years later – when Kohler took a cast-iron horse trough, heated it to 1,700 degrees F, sprinkled it with enamel powder and added legs to make it into a bathtub – that the company made its mark in the home plumbing products market.

John Michael Kohler later built a new foundry four miles inland from Sheboygan, which began production in the fall of 1900. The 21-acre property was located at the intersection of two trails used by the local Native American tribes. Farmsteads sprung up near the factory. The settlement incorporated as the Village of Kohler in 1912 and became one of the first planned communities in the United States.

Fast-forward two generations, and Herb Kohler Jr. succeeds his father as chief executive officer in 1972 and president in 1974. Under his leadership, the Kohler Company has grown to generate nearly $6 billion in annual revenue with more than fifty manufacturing facilities around the world. The company employs approximately 32,000 people within four distinct business groups: Kitchen & Bath, Interiors, Global Power, and Hospitality & Real Estate.

As a young man, Kohler hatched the idea of setting aside some land the company had acquired around the village over the years. He proposed designating a particular area as a preserve and calling it River Wildlife and Recreation. The idea didn't go anywhere at the time, but Kohler resurrected the concept twenty years later when he held a more influential position as leader of the company.

This time, the idea took off and the company designated eight hundred wooded acres in the nearby Sheboygan River valley for a private club to be known as River Wildlife. Part of the property became a recreational retreat with a variety of outdoor activities. Its popularity and financial success encouraged Kohler to move toward additional ways of incorporating sports and recreation into his company's business model.

The Sports Core sports and fitness facility soon opened for employees and the public, while at the same time, Kohler began looking into modern uses for the old American Club building. The former dorm stood across the street from the factory and originally housed single male immigrant employees when it opened in 1918.

Renovating the historic building wasn't at the top of the list of pet projects for some members of the company's board of directors. Eventually, however, they warmed to the idea of transforming the building into a world-class hotel. The American Club opened in 1981 after a three-year renovation effort and soon earned the American Automobile Association's prestigious Five Diamond designation. It is the only hotel in the Midwest to hold that distinction.

World-class golf was the next logical extension of the hospitality business. Kohler enlisted the assistance of his company's then-vice president of business development, Bob Milbourne, a very good golfer in his own right. The two men determined the best place to site a golf course was adjacent to the forest of the River Wildlife sanctuary, the site of today's Blackwolf Run courses.

The rest, as they say, is history. Kohler selected Pete Dye to design the first Blackwolf Run course, which opened in 1988. If you haven't done so already, go back and read Pete Dye's foreword to this book for additional insight into the story of their collaboration.

Demand for tee times soon outpaced supply, spurred by national exposure in being named Best New Public Course of 1988 by *Golf Digest*. Kohler brought Dye back to Eastern Wisconsin on numerous occasions to expand on what had become an extremely popular golf offering. The courses at Blackwolf Run and Whistling Straits soon caught the eye of the United

States Golf Association (USGA) and the Professional Golfers Association (PGA), which awarded numerous major championships to the Kohler venues. Whistling Straits will host the Ryder Cup matches in 2020, and a fifth course south of Sheboygan is in the planning stages as of this writing.

Herb Kohler stepped down from his role as CEO as of June 1, 2015, yielding the chair to his son, David Kohler. The elder Kohler continues to oversee the board of directors, lead its executive committee, oversee shareholder communications, and manage mergers and acquisitions along with the hospitality and real estate group. Of course, the latter includes the company's golf courses in Wisconsin and the United Kingdom.

For someone who had little interest in golf into middle age, Herb Kohler has created a legacy that will make Eastern Wisconsin a prime golf destination for as long as the game is played.

*Golf in Eastern Wisconsin*

*Golf in Eastern Wisconsin*

# Whistling Straits
# The Straits Course

*Haven, Wisconsin*

We might as well start out with the star of the show. After all, this Pete Dye masterpiece is one of the main reasons you're looking at this book right now, isn't it?

There's a reason – well, many reasons – why the Straits consistently ranks among the top few public courses in the USA. From the beauty of Lake Michigan, almost always your companion around this north-south layout, to the eye-popping visuals Dye created from mountains of sand brought in to construct the course, the Straits quickly shot to fame as the host of multiple major championships including the 2004, 2010 and 2015 PGA Championships, the 2007 U.S. Senior Open, and the 2020 Ryder Cup.

The presence of fescue fairways with wispy rough is unusual in the Upper Midwest and adds to the links feel of this unique course. Caddies are required at the Straits (except during twilight play) and add to the enjoyment of the round. Give your caddie an honest overview of your game and approximate club distances, and they'll be able to suggest the best strategies to navigate your loop.

All of the more than one thousand sand traps play as waste bunkers, meaning you can ground your club without penalty and will encounter more footprints than you're likely accustomed to seeing at your home course. Only during Tour play are the traps played as hazards. Recall Dustin Johnson's unfortunate penalty for grounding his club in a fairway bunker on No. 18, keeping him out of a playoff at the 2010 PGA Championship.

Choosing the correct set of tees for your ability level is paramount to enjoying your round. As you can see from the course ratings below, even the middle "Green" tees feature a Slope rating north of 140. That should tell you something about the difficulty of this course. Unless you are a Tour-caliber player, the black tees shouldn't be more than a source of chuckles as you walk past them on your way forward.

With that said, let the adventure begin!

**The Straits Course**
**Men's Yardages, Rating and Slope**
Black – 7,790 yards – 77.2/152
Blue – 7,142 yards – 74.2/145
Green – 6,663 yards – 71.9/141
White – 6,360 yards – 70.4/137
Red – 5,564 yards – 66.4/129

**Ladies' Yardages, Rating and Slope**
Green – 6,663 yards – 79.4/143
White – 6,360 yards – 76.9/137
Red – 5,564 yards – 72.7/129

**Hole Yardages (Black/Blue/Green/White/Red)**

**No. 1 – Par 4**
(493/405/370/361/325)

The visual intimidation factor is high for most players here. Even the walk from the staging area, down through a creek valley and up to the first tee provides a panoramic vista unlike anything you've seen before. It's not every day you see dunes and sand traps as far as the eye can see. If you're not careful, it's easy to fall into the mental trap of, "Where *can* I hit it?"

Take a deep breath, swing within yourself and enjoy the day, regardless of your score. Pete Dye may have presented you with one of the most difficult, dramatic courses in the world, but "Outward Bound" doesn't have to be a round-killer right off the bat. In fact, this modest opener ranks as the easiest hole that's not a par-3 on the front nine.

As with virtually every hole on the Straits, choice of tee set and playing ability will determine your strategy. The hole doglegs left around a long, irregular bunker set below the level of the fairway. A bunker on the right-center as you view the slightly uphill landing area serves as your target. It begins about 130 yards from the front of the green.

Favoring the right side steers you clear of the trouble left and sets up a short- to mid-iron approach with a more open angle to the green. Missing right on the approach is preferable to finding the pot bunkers left and below the putting surface. Shots that land short and right have a chance to kick onto the green as Lake Michigan makes its appearance with a dramatic backdrop.

## No. 2 – Par 5
(597/533/521/508/447)

Your heart rate likely still is elevated, but walking the course is helping you settle into a rhythm. That's good, because you'll need to put a couple of good swings on the ball here to take advantage of this good scoring opportunity.

"Cross Country" plays south, with the lake to your left the entire trip. The hole runs along a plateau above and just inland from the seventh and eighth holes. A tee shot down the left side of the fairway brings a dropoff and sand into play, but it's necessary to gain a sightline for your second shot. The fairway turns right just enough about 250 yards from the green that the high mounds defining a large bunker on the right can block your view.

It's also possible for bigger hitters to drive past that point and set up an opportunity to reach the green in two. Keep in mind that missing the fairway here virtually guarantees your next shot will be out of a waste bunker. Dye left a little room for error in the left rough for players blocked by the high mounds on the right. This wider area runs for a 100-yard stretch leading up to the 150 mark, creating an opportunity to recover from a wayward tee shot and still have a chance at hitting the green in regulation.

The landing area for the second shot is a challenging target. The fairway narrows considerably about 115 yards from the green before heading slightly uphill to your destination. Missing left that final 100 yards is not the place to be, with sand and rough waiting well below the level of the green.

A pot bunker 35 yards short and right of the green acts like a magnet in capturing balls that appear to be on a good line toward the green or the safe runoff zone to the right. Note the pin placement on this 35-yard deep putting surface when sizing up your approach, and just make sure you don't miss left.

## No. 3 – Par 3
(188/180/166/154/111)

This fun little hole ranks as the easiest handicap hole on the front nine. If played correctly, you have a good chance at par or better. However, as with any hole at the Straits, a poor shot can spell disaster faster than you can say "O'Man."

While pin position is an important consideration on a green that's 43 yards deep, your target should always be right of the flag. The green slopes severely to the left, particularly off a hump midway into the putting surface. Shots typically release down the slope and move left. A steep face leading up to the green requires shots toward front pin positions carry all the way to the putting surface.

The green sits at an angle, with back left pin positions appearing to perch on a sliver of grass hanging out over Lake Michigan. Anything pulled left will find bunkers or gnarly rough well below the green – if you're lucky. One bad kick off the bank could send your ball all the way to the lakeshore.

Let your caddie read your putt for you. Perhaps nowhere on the Straits is local knowledge more helpful than putting on this green.

*The par-4 fourth at Whistling Straits (Photo courtesy Kohler Co.)*

## No. 4 – Par 4
(494/451/414/404/354)

The final hole of the front nine's southward stretch is a doozy. The No. 1 handicap hole on the card, "Glory" is a long par-4 that requires length and accuracy. While not necessarily a hole that will ruin your round – although it certainly can – bogeys and doubles far outnumber pars.

The tee shot is the key to having any chance. The fairway sits at a slight angle from right to left and slopes slightly to the left. Large dunes and bunkers down the right side will catch your eye, but there is more of the same below the level of the fairway down the left.

A bunker complex on the right pinches the fairway in the landing area about 160 yards from the green. If conditions are favorable, it's possible to skirt the left side of the fairway and roll out down a hill into a wide collection area. The good news is you're now closer to the green and on short grass. The bad news is you could be below the level of the green with a more difficult angle over the large bunkers short and left of the putting surface.

If you leave yourself in a bad spot after your tee shot, keep in mind the fairway narrows a second time about 75 yards short of the green. There is another safe landing area about 50 yards short and right of the green, but you will have to gauge the risk compared to just laying back to 100 yards and hitting in from there.

Up at the green, left is absolutely dead. Consider yourself lucky to find the bunkers; otherwise, you could bounce all the way down to the lake. Dye left a generous bailout area short and right of the long putting surface. Mounding on the right may even kick your ball onto the green. Make par here and you'll likely walk away with a skin.

## No. 5 – Par 5
(603/563/543/527/459)

Regardless of your length off the tee, convince yourself to play "Snake" as a three-shot hole. The risks are just too high to do anything but play smart. Vijay Singh reached this green in two when he won the PGA Championship here in 2004, but even by Tour standards that was incredible.

The tee shot plays into the prevailing wind and should favor the left side, away from bunkers and a water hazard that form the dogleg. The hole turns 90 degrees right at this point, with more water defining the left side the rest of the way and bunkers continuing down the right.

Most players will need to rely on the experience of their caddie to pick out a target for their second shot. Mounds within the field of bunkers that form the dogleg will block your view of the fairway beyond. It takes a high level commitment to aim for a target you can't see, but trust your caddie and you will put yourself in position to score.

The farther you can advance your second shot down the fairway, the more the green opens up for your approach. The green wraps back around the water hazard to the left, with a beach-type bunker framing the front and left. There is bailout room to the right of the green, but not over the back.

## No. 6 – Par 4
(409/378/360/352/282)

"Gremlin's Ear" is a short par-4 that demands a tee shot anywhere but right. Coming on the heels of two very difficult holes, the sixth should provide an opportunity to steady the ship.

*Your short game will receive a severe test should you miss the green on the par-4 sixth at Whistling Straits. (Photo courtesy Kohler Co.)*

When the wind is favorable, big hitters can even take a crack at reaching the front left of the green. For the rest of us, pick a target down the left side and perhaps consider swinging something less than a driver.

A pot bunker down the left side of the fairway about 150 yards from the green is a good target. Any shot just right of that bunker or beyond is good. Dye left a generous area of rough beyond and left of the bunker that isn't a bad place to be if you miss the fairway.

Missing right is another story. Challenging stances, brutal rough and a series of bunkers set below the level of the fairway are very difficult to say the least. Second shots hit from down there require all carry back up the hill to reach the putting surface.

A bunker on the right side of the fairway about 80 yards from the center of the green features a high brow that can affect your sight line to the target. Beyond that bunker, the hillside pitches dramatically downward into a large bowl dotted with bunkers and more unmaintained rough leading to the green. Don't be surprised if you detect a groan from your caddie should you hit one down there. They've seen too many players waste too many shots there; plus, the terrain is treacherous.

The green is exceptionally wide and fairly shallow, divided by a deep bunker that pushes into the front of putting surface with a significant mound. Depending on your angle of attack, pin position can make a major difference in yardage for your approach. Long is preferable to leaving it short. Your caddie will laser your yardage and put you in position to score.

## No. 7 – Par 3
(221/205/185/172/132)

Get your camera ready for one of the most photographed holes in North America. "Shipwreck" is a strong par-3 with severe penalty for missing the large green.

The hole is layered into the shoreline with Lake Michigan on the right and towering dunes to the left. The lake provides an obvious hazard, but bailing out to the left may not provide much relief. A series of bunkers cut into the hillside above the green leaves a downhill pitch, making it easy for balls to run right through to the opposite rough.

A large bunker short of the green shouldn't come into play, but the bunkers below and right that separate the green from the lake get plenty of action. Be aware that you may not feel the wind from the tee because of the shelter from the dunes.

The green is 42 yards deep, requiring a good yardage from your caddie for club selection. You can be more aggressive with pin positions on the front left; otherwise, the middle of the green is a good place to be.

## No. 8 – Par 4
(506/470/429/405/355)

"On the Rocks" is the last place you want to be on this very strong par-4. A blind tee shot to an elevated fairway must stay left of the quarter-mile of terror that lurks below the ridge bordering the entire right side of this dogleg-right hole.

Your caddie will give you a line that's likely farther left than you might guess, but trust him on this. The fairway pinches down the right for well-struck tee shots, meaning it's possible to run out of fairway and drop off into a deep valley of doom if you're not careful.

A triangle-shaped bunker complex sticks its nose into the fairway on the left side of the landing area about 150 yards from the front of the green. Although finding the sand there isn't ideal, it still is preferable to missing the fairway right.

The approach features one of the best views on the course, slightly downhill with the lake behind the green. The open front allows run-up shots as long as you avoid the deep bunker short and left of the green. The putting surface is exceptionally long at 47 yards, meaning club selection could vary dramatically. Plan for some run-out on your approach, particularly if you're coming in with a long club.

Dye left some chipping areas short and left of the green, so take advantage of his generosity and avoid missing right at all costs.

### No. 9 – Par 4
(442/412/384/371/347)

One of the easier driving holes on the course, "Down and Dirty" grows its teeth for the approach shot.

If you're a long hitter, you may want to swing something less than a driver to stay short of a bunker that narrows the fairway at the far end of the landing zone. This hole often plays into the prevailing wind, and the fairway tilts slightly toward the right. Tee shots that leak too far right may leave you partially blocked by a large tree that sits at the crest of the hill about 100 yards short of the green.

The green sits in the Seven Mile Creek valley in a natural amphitheater below the clubhouse. This can create some swirling wind conditions, encouraging a lower-trajectory approach shot to control the flight.

The only safe place to miss is short of this relatively narrow green. A thin bunker is all that separates the front-right portion of the green from the creek. One bad bounce or a shot more than just a little off target will find that hazard.

Remember to grab a brat on your way to the tenth tee and prepare for an incredible back nine.

### No. 10 – Par 4
(391/376/334/320/304)

There are precious few opportunities to score on the inward nine at the Straits – especially once you reach the final few holes – so you have to take advantage of them when they occur. "Voyageur" is a funky little hole that offers one such chance.

Despite its modest yardage, driver is the play here to set up a short-iron approach to the table-top green. A yawning bunker in the middle of the fairway appears even larger thanks to the wide collar of rough that surrounds it. The visual impact of this bunker is magnified by the fact it sits into the uphill slope of the fairway, staring you in the face as you pick out your line.

Take your caddie's advice on your line. By now he'll have a good feel for whether you can go for a little glory left of that bunker or play it safe and hit to the fatter part of the fairway to the right. Bigger hitters can take it right over that bunker, too.

Choosing the right-side option makes the hole play longer, but the green still should be reachable. The left side offers the shorter route, with its main risk being the rough below the level of the fairway. Keep in mind that regardless of your path, the approach is significantly uphill and you'll need an extra club to make the climb.

For those who miss the fairway left off the tee, your penalty is a difficult stance from a steep hillside and all carry up the hill to the green. Anything short from there finds its way to a collection area a good thirty feet below the green.

The green angles from front right to back left, with the back-left portion sloping away. Prepare for some rollout when going after those back pin positions. Approach shots short of the green likely will kick left and down the hill, leaving a very difficult pitch back up to the putting surface.

There are plenty of opportunities to find trouble here, but anytime Pete Dye gives you the chance to put a short iron in your hand for the approach, you need to take advantage of it.

## No. 11 – Par 5
(645/563/544/519/479)

It's relatively unusual for a par-5 to rank as one of the more difficult handicap holes, but "Sand Box" is the third-hardest hole on the back nine for a reason. In addition to the obvious distance requirement, there is plenty that can go wrong along the way to make your arrival at the green a challenging trek.

Go ahead and swing away off the tee. You'll need all the distance you can get. Just make sure you avoid missing the fairway right, where a series of dunes, bunkers and rough will rob you of distance and put pressure on your second shot. A south wind and a big drive give longer players a chance to get home in two.

Most players hit their second shots down a hill and into a valley next to the hole's signature feature: an enormous, deep bunker defining the left side that begins about 100 yards from the green. Dye's famous railroad ties are set vertically to shore up the walls of this cavernous pit. Players of lesser ability will find it difficult even getting out of this predicament.

The fairway holds its own challenge. The third shot from the valley is blind, played up the hill to a crowned green that repels as many shots as it accepts. If you have the length to get your second shot up on top of the plateau, short of the green and right of the big bunker, your mission becomes much easier.

Large chipping areas surround the putting surface, and bunkers front right and back center see their share of visitors. A false front makes it necessary to carry all the way to the green. It's not an impossible hole, but certainly one that requires three good shots to walk away with a good score.

*Pete Dye's famous railroad ties support the walls of this incredible bunker leading to the eleventh green at Whistling Straits. (Photo courtesy Kohler Co.)*

## No. 12 – Par 3
(163/138/118/99/89)

"Pop Up" is a confounding little hole that creates its share of frustration. You'd think a hole that requires only a short iron wouldn't be that difficult, and it isn't in many instances. However, put the pin in the center or back-right portions of this green and it becomes grip-squeezingly treacherous. Anything short or right kicks down a steep hill toward bunkers and Lake Michigan.

The green is exceptionally long and angles from front left to back right. In reality, it plays like two separate greens. The front left target is by far the easiest, with the largest square footage and most receptive green contours. Get the right yardage from your caddie and it may be nothing more than a flip wedge.

Pins set in the narrower middle section bring a front bunker into play that features a hump sloping away from the tee. Most shots that land on that slope kick forward, over the green and into a difficult position to get up and down. Most players are better off aiming for the fat part of the green left of that position and taking their chances with the putter.

The right-side pin positions are almost humorous. "Oh, c'mon," is a common reaction when players walk up to the tee and see that target. This section of the green is tiny and any miss is trouble. Discuss with your caddie whether it's worth going for this part of the green or not. You may be better off playing safe and hoping for a good lag putt.

But you didn't come all this way and pay all that money just to play safe, did you?

## No. 13 – Par 4
(402/389/364/336/319)

The next two holes provide your last best chances for scoring, at least according to the handicap rankings. If you can play this section well and have a few shots in hand, it certainly will make the stretch run a little less stressful. That doesn't mean to imply these holes are a cakewalk, however.

"Cliff Hanger" is a beautiful, short par-4 that rewards accuracy more than brawn. A slight left-to-right shape off the tee will follow the contour of the fairway and roll toward the green. A good target for that shot is just left of the volcano-like bunker on the left side of the fairway.

Don't overcook it, though, because right of the fairway is not good. The hillside slopes toward Lake Michigan on the right, with layers of bunkers terraced into the hill. An approach shot from this position invites trouble.

The fairway begins to narrow about 100 yards from the green. For this reason, bigger hitters with a favorable wind may choose to swing something less than driver from the tee.

The approach looks down on a green perched over the shoreline. Anything right or long gets wet. The green is open in front, with a chipping area and a lone bunker in a collection area left of the putting surface.

This green and the next tee are at the far northern end of the property; time to make the turn and head back home. Before you do, take a moment to appreciate the view. On my last visit to the Straits, our group had to wait here for the course's black-faced sheep to pile over the dunes and walk purposefully across the green, leaving droppings along the way. We just looked at each other with a smile and said, "How cool is this?"

## No. 14 – Par 4
(396/360/346/332/271)

"Widow's Watch" seemingly invites a right-to-left shot shape to take advantage of the matching slope of the fairway and the dogleg-left design. To some extent, that strategy can work; however, the lower level of the fairway can leave a blind second shot. Tall mounds within the large bunker complex that defines the dogleg's elbow block your vision to the green unless your drive travels well down the fairway.

Leaving your tee shot at least partway up the hill gives you a look at the green. Now all you have to do is negotiate the downhill lie with a relatively short iron. Nothing will ever be easy, but this is the preferred option.

The shortness of the hole invites something less than a driver off the tee, but it's to your benefit to get as far down the fairway as you can. The fairway narrows at the dogleg, so there is an amount of risk to an aggressive strategy. However, that removes the risk of having a blind second shot.

The approach into the green is more open from back in the fairway. The green angles from front left to back right, with a severe bunker complex guarding the right side. The farther down the fairway you hit your drive, the more that complex becomes something you need to carry, especially for right side/back pin positions.

The green features one of the more undulating putting surfaces on the course, complete with distinct shelves and in-green backstops. Your caddie will be of help in giving you an appropriate target.

## No. 15 – Par 4
(503/464/429/402/367)

Well, here we go. The next four holes command even the Tour pros' attention. The finishing stretch at the Straits isn't about making birdies; it's about survival and avoiding disaster. It's about playing smart and taking your caddie's advice.

"Grand Strand" is a strong par-4 that demands you challenge the narrowing fairway in the landing zone. The fairway sets up for a slight left-to-right shot shape, but honestly, that's a minor consideration for most players. Do anything you have to and just put the ball in play.

The bunker complexes on both sides of the fairway are no treat to hit from, and a cross-bunker 90 yards from the green will catch shots running on the ground. Favor the right side on your approach, where there is better chipping access. You can't tell from back in the fairway, but there is some room over the green as Lake Michigan provides a stunning backdrop.

The approach to the green is open in front and accepts longer shots that bounce onto the putting surface. The green features many subtle breaks that make putting a challenge.

**No. 16 – Par 5**
(568/545/535/513/412)

Par-5s typically offer the best opportunities to score, and "Endless Bite" is no exception. Blast away off the tee, taking care to avoid the rugged stretch of bunkers below the fairway to the left. The fairway tilts slightly that direction, so plan for a little rollout.

A large bunker complex that impinges on the right side of fairway is out of range for most players. If you're able to get it out that far, you have a decision to make about how aggressive you want to be with your second shot.

It's about 240 yards to the front of the green from there, and the route to glory requires all carry over a cutout on the left side. A miss short or left leaves you well below the level of the green amidst layers of dunes, bunkers and rough. Recall that in the final round of the 2010 PGA Championship, Dustin Johnson left his second shot down the bluff left of the green, and then made a miraculous pitch to tap-in range for birdie. Most of us don't possess those skills.

Minus that kind of length, Dye has left plenty of room to play conservatively down the right side and set up a short third into the green. There is more room beyond the right-side fairway bunker complex than it appears, as the fairway swings around to the right. You will have a better view for your third shot if you can put your second on top of the plateau that begins about 70 yards from the green.

The green sits on a precipice overlooking the lake, which understandably makes it difficult to go after back pin positions. There is a little room off the right and back-right portions of the green for chipping, but nothing long and left.

**No. 17 – Par 3**
(249/223/197/165/131)

It doesn't take a rocket scientist to realize left is not the place to be on "Pinched Nerve." This long, beautiful par-3 (pictured on the front cover) is one of Pete Dye's most difficult short holes in the world. Vertical railroad ties support the green short and left, providing an additional visual intimidation factor.

The green is quite deep at 43 yards in length, and there is more room to the right than you can see from the tee. A large, elevated bunker short right of the green creates a dramatic balance to the dropoff to the lake on the left. It also blocks the view of the far right portion of the putting surface.

Playing too safely and missing the green right is no picnic par save, either. The approach to the green is open and flat, so don't discount that as a viable option. Favor the right-center of the green regardless of the pin position and take your chances with the putter. Par here will feel like a birdie.

**No. 18 – Par 4**
(520/487/424/420/380)

I hope you have a shot in hand heading into "Dyeabolical," because this phenomenal hole plays as a par-5 for many players due to the long forced carry over Seven Mile Creek to reach the green.

As you walk to the tee from the seventeenth green, take a glance back to the left and check out the championship tee boxes. They're rather humorous, actually. Playing from the upper sets of tees on the right, you have a straighter look right down the fairway.

Longer hitters need to account for significant rollout down the hill. Depending on the wind, may want to hit something less than driver to ensure you don't run out of fairway. Yes, Dustin Johnson's famous penalty bunker that kept him out of the PGA Championship playoff is on the right.

The creek valley cuts a serpentine route to the left and in front of the left portion of the green. There is plenty of fairway across the valley and up the right side all the way to the green. Take advantage of that safety net and play this as a three-shot hole if you aren't in position, or don't have the length, to challenge the hazard all the way to the green.

You will be hitting downhill to a huge green set in the amphitheater below the clubhouse. As if the shot isn't difficult enough, the wind swirls down there, typically requiring an extra club for the distance at hand.

The massive green is 44 yards deep and features numerous lobes with dozens of possible pin positions. Make sure you get a good yardage from your caddie before making your club decision. This is an example of where a laser device is worth its weight in gold.

If you're able to make par here – whether that's 4 or 5 in your mind – walk up the hill with your head held high. Congratulations, you are in the minority of players to successfully navigate one of the great home holes in all of golf.

**Summary**

The Straits course lives up to its billing as one of the most spectacular courses in North America, if not the world. Pete Dye offers a nice mix of lengths, greens complexes and imaginative bunkering, and even the so-called easy holes present the potential for disaster. If this course is on your bucket list, you won't be disappointed.

*Golf in Eastern Wisconsin*

# Whistling Straits
# The Irish Course

*Haven, Wisconsin*

If it wasn't for the presence of the Straits Course on the same property, the Irish Course might be hailed as one of Pete Dye's more dramatic projects. The Irish isn't quite as difficult as its big brother and has bentgrass fairways instead of fescue; differences which make it the perfect companion for a 36-hole visit. However, don't let that description lull you into a false sense of security. The Irish is a lot of golf course and does not yield low scores for many first-time visitors.

Although the Straits Course gets its share of publicity for the incredible number of bunkers that dot the layout, the Irish isn't exactly devoid of sand. In fact, if the Straits has the most sand traps of any course in the world, the Irish may run a close second. All sand traps play as waste bunkers on both the Irish and Straits courses. This means it's within the rules to ground your club and footprints may be plentiful, depending on how late in the day you play.

Riding carts are available at the Irish, but the cart path-only format usually leaves you walking just as many steps as if you used a caddie. The professional caddies at the two Straits courses know every blade of grass, lines to blind landing areas and tendencies of the greens, and they certainly add to the enjoyment of the day. I have been fortunate to have veteran looper Charlie Spain on my bag for a couple of rounds over the years, and I can vouch for the fact a professional caddie is worth their weight in gold. Treat yourself to a caddie; you'll be glad you did.

**The Irish Course**
**Men's Yardages, Rating and Slope**
Black – 7,201 yards – 75.6/146
Blue – 6,750 yards – 73.5/141
Green – 6,366 yards – 72.0/137
White – 5,992 yards – 70.3/133
Red – 5,109 yards – 65.6/121

**Ladies' Yardages, Rating and Slope**
Green – 6,366 yards – 77.4/142
White – 5,992 yards – 75.2/137
Red – 5,109 yards – 70.0/126

**Hole Yardages (Black/Blue/Green/White/Red)**

**No. 1 – Par 4**
(400/387/369/359/301)

"High Ground" is listed as the second-hardest handicap hole on the outward nine, but in reality, the most difficult aspect of the opening hole may be your nerves. The generous fairway provides ample opportunity to get off to a good start, with the right side providing the best angle to the green. Pete Dye even offers a little more room behind a mounded bunker at the beginning of the fairway down the right side than it appears to allow for that extra few pounds of grip pressure.

Go ahead and blast away from the tee. There is plenty of uphill yardage before the fairway narrows 90 yards from the green. A deep grass bunker begins 75 yards short and left of the green, with your first look at the sand and fescue-covered mounds that await most errant approach shots.

The only safe miss is short and right, and the green slopes toward the left bunkers. It's possible to putt or chip right off the front of the green if you're a little too frisky. Remember to breathe, and you just might walk away from here with a par.

*The short, par-4 second on the Irish Course gives you plenty of incentive to stay right. (Photo courtesy Kohler Co.)*

**No. 2 – Par 4**
(372/360/347/340/309)

In typical Pete Dye fashion, "Giant's Leap" plays with your mind to make a moderate hole look much more difficult than it should be. The view from tee to green is completely over water. But look over there to the right –

there's a wide fairway waiting for you that doesn't even require a driver for good position.

The fairway gently turns to the left around the pond, and the best approach angles come from nearer the water. Since this should be nothing more than a short- to mid-iron approach for most players, the smart play is toward a mound about 20 yards right of a bunker that frames the right side of the fairway. That bunker is about 70 yards from the green, meaning it shouldn't be in play.

Two small bunkers in front and another behind provide an intimidating visual. The green is elevated just enough to make it look even more shallow from the fairway than it is. A miss right of the green is safe, while left and long is not. Trust your yardage, and two good swings give you a chance at par.

**No. 3 – Par 3**
(147/138/128/118/87)

Look at all the railroad ties fronting the green. Dye placed his trademark woodwork vertically along a transition between the level of the green and a sliver of sand that separates it from a water hazard. The result adds a visually appealing aspect to a relatively easy hole.

"Sleeper" is the shortest hole on the course and the No. 18 handicap on the card, meaning this little beauty theoretically is your best chance at par or birdie. The green angles from front right to back left, with left-side pin positions presenting the most challenge.

Pull your approach or hit it a little fat, and you bring the hazards into play. A large hump works into the putting surface off a bunker right of the green, making putts in that portion especially treacherous. Pay attention to the pin position, as it can make as much as a three-club difference in club selection.

**No. 4 – Par 4**
(489/443/432/405/336)

"Sandbanks" ranks as the most difficult handicap hole on the front nine for a reason. If the length doesn't get your attention, perhaps the 165-yard-long bunker that highlights the left side of this sweeping dogleg-left brute will catch your eye. Another large bunker on the opposite side of the fairway, while not as visually evident as its left-side partner, catches its share of tee shots as well.

The landing area narrows considerably the more you attempt to bite off the dogleg. The line off the tee is toward the right side of an opening visible in the far tree line. Consult your yardage guide or your caddie to see what your approximate carry yardage is to reach the fairway. Cut too much off the corner and you will face a 200-yard sand shot, which is not a specialty for most players.

The open front to the green allows run-up shots and is the only safe place to miss. Bunkers and mounds populate the landscape everywhere else, including a huge sand trap that covers the final 90 yards leading up the right side.

There are two major features on the green worth mentioning. The first is a large mound toward the back-left that influences putts and the typically long approach shots that come in hot. The second is a back-right tail of the green that curls beyond the large greenside bunker complex. The best way to access that part of the green is to hit a runner that catches the contour and releases to the back. Par earns a skin here more often than not.

## No. 5 – Par 5
(570/517/501/477/430)

Decisions, decisions. Dye loves his par-5s to have risk/reward characteristics, especially when the risk may not produce as much reward as first appears. That's the case on several par-5s at The Irish.

"Devil's Elbow" doglegs right nearly 90 degrees around a large bunker at the elbow. The conservative play – and the smart play in most instances – is straight down the fairway left of that bunker. However, if the wind conditions are favorable, bigger hitters can have a go at cutting the dogleg and making this a two-shot hole. The payoff is an iron to the green if you're able to pull it off.

If you want to give that a try, make sure you don't stray any further right than the tree line, because anything right of that is gone. Players with serious length can take it just right of the tree line from the green or blue tees, but not much. Your caddie will know your game well enough by this point to advise you correctly.

For the rest of us mortals, the safe play down the fairway leaves a risk/reward decision for the second shot as well. A layup leaves you well back from the green, between 140 and 170 yards depending on your aggressiveness. The fairway grows increasingly narrow as it approaches a crossing water hazard. Bunkers guard both sides of that landing area and the cart path crosses at the end of the fairway, sometimes assisting balls into the creek.

Attempting to carry that hazard is no sure thing, especially for higher handicappers. A flight of at least 175 yards is needed to find a narrow, mounded fairway that angles right to left toward a long, narrow green. More of Dye's vertical railroad ties front the fairway on the opposite side of the hazard, and sand follows the hole up the left side all the way to the green.

A tall flagpole behind the green and to the right can help you gauge the wind. The green is open at the front and curves around to the back left. Unless you have a short iron in your hand, play to the fat of the green for back-left pin positions.

*The par-3 sixth at the Irish Course plays to an island green in a sea of sand. (Photo courtesy of Kohler Co.)*

## No. 6 – Par 3
(160/149/135/123)

"Mulligan's Watch" shouldn't be a difficult hole. After all, it's less than 150 yards from everywhere forward of the back tees. However, sand surrounds this island green and tends to tighten the grip pressure a bit. Dye also layered a beach-full of bunkers into the mounds that are not even close to being in play, but anything to mess with your head adds to the fun.

Remember that all traps are waste bunkers at the Irish, meaning the sand depth often is quite shallow. The blast shot you may be used to playing at your home course isn't always an option here, and this hole is a perfect example of that.

The green itself is fairly flat, so par is a good possibility if your tee shot finds green grass.

## No. 7 – Par 4
(372/363/344/339/320)

Discretion is the better part of valor on "Troll," as position is more important than length. A large, built-up bunker dominates the right side of the landing area. The hole doglegs right past the bunker, but there is no benefit from driving past it. The fairway narrows and a hazard pinches in from the right beyond this point. Right of the fairway is dead the entire length of the hole.

The wide fairway offers two options, each with its pros and cons. Left of the bunker adds distance to the approach and presents a broader target at the green. However, the shallow green depth from that angle requires precise distance control with the penalty a difficult save. The right side of the fairway is significantly lower than the left and can result in a blind second shot. The benefit is a shorter club in your hand with a better angle to the green, a combination capable of producing more short birdie putts than approaching from the left.

Depending on your length, your caddie may recommend something less than a driver off the tee. You'll also benefit from leaving enough distance to put a full swing on your approach and impart the spin needed to hold the relatively shallow green.

The green curves around to the left, with more putting surface and a chipping area available beyond the high-faced bunker that forms the elbow of the green's shape. This enhances the advantage of approaching from the right side of the fairway. The back left portion is higher than the front right. Find the correct level of the green, and you will have a shot at birdie here.

## No. 8 – Par 5
(555/542/501/459/392)

Big hitters who can crank up a power fade off the tee might be able to shrink "Garden Creek" into a two-shot hole. A speed slot down the right-center of the fairway around the corner adds some extra rollout, but you have to be pretty large to take advantage of that design feature.

For the rest of us, anything in the short grass is a good place to be. This sets up a risk/reward decision for the second shot. Do you blast away and flirt with the bunker in the middle of the fairway about 50 yards short of the green? Or do you lay up farther back on the left side, taking the bunker and a hazard on the right side out of play?

The approach to the green is uphill all the way from the creek, making depth perception difficult. The green is deep and angles from front right to back left. Short and right is the best chipping zone. From the popular layup zone 100 yards short of the green, back-left pin positions require all carry over a large bunker. A collection of bunkers set above and into the hillside frame this attractive target.

**No. 9 – Par 4**
(484/409/322/308/263)

Your choice of tee makes a big difference in how you'll navigate "Last Gaspe." There is nearly a 180-yard difference between the black and white tees! An S-shaped creek crosses the fairway in the landing area, requiring a much longer carry to reach safety down the center and left than it does down the right side.

You have no choice but to lay up short of the creek from the black tee, while carrying the hazard is possible from the blue tee down the right side of the fairway. Consult your yardage guide and your caddie for specific carry distances.

A driver is too much for most players from any of the forward tee sets, as the creek crosses the fairway again about 70 yards short of the green. The green is deeper than it appears, so take note of the pin position when hitting your approach.

Quick tip: Take a look at the eighteenth green as you leave the ninth hole and walk over to the tenth tee. You won't have a good look at this pin position and general lay of the land from the fairway below later on.

**No. 10 – Par 4**
(398/387/378/361/340)

The beautiful, uphill "Shepherd's Post" begins your trek to the northern part of the course. It is imperative to hit this fairway to have a good chance of making par. A miss left sends you down an embankment and into rough and sand, while right features irregularly shaped bunkers layered into the mounds.

Despite the hole's moderate length, don't be afraid to hit driver off the tee. The uphill slope will minimize your rollout, and the fairway retains its generous width all the way up to the green. The only safe approach miss is short, but a severe slope will kick balls to the left and down a hill to a collection area well below the green.

The blind green angles around a bunker from front right to back left. A low area behind catches shots that roll through the putting surface, leaving a very difficult up and down if the pin is in the back portion. Par is more uncommon here than you might think.

*The sweeping tenth fairway at the Irish Course leads uphill to a plateau green. (Photo courtesy Kohler Co.)*

## No. 11 – Par 3
(208/193/177/169/125)

The most important variable hitting into this 50-yard-long green is club selection. "Lamb Chop" features a bunker that begins at the tee and follows all the way to the front of the green and along the right side.

If you're going to miss, the right side isn't really that bad of a place to be. There is a narrow strip of grass between the bunker and the steep bank leading to the green. A miss left is potentially more penal, bringing into play a pair of bunkers with nine-foot faces to block your path back to safety.

The fat of the green is never a bad place to be here as long as your club selection leaves you in the same zip code as the pin. This is a good opportunity for par.

## No. 12 – Par 4
(413/396/373/349/290)

This unusually straight par-4 for a Dye design doesn't come without its quirks. "Highland Trek" appears benign enough from the tee with its generous fairway – in fact, it ranks as the easiest hole that's not a par-3 on the back nine – but woe unto those with a tendency to hit it left, because you may not see your playing partners again until the green. Your caddie won't be too pleased with you, either.

By the time your ball finishes bouncing down the steep slope that defines the entire left side of the hole, you can find yourself up to 25 feet below the surface of the fairway or green. Mounds down the right create a natural tendency to play down the center and take advantage of the wide landing area. The problem with that strategy is the second shot will be all carry over the valley where it cuts into the fairway just short of the green.

Instead, the optimal line off the tee is actually down the right rough. The fairway angles right slightly beyond some mounds, and the general left slope of the hole kicks balls back toward the fairway. The resulting approach shot avoids a good portion of the valley of death and creates a relatively straightforward approach to a long green that opens up to your position.

If the angle is in your favor, the open front of the green is receptive to shots that bounce onto the putting surface.

## No. 13 – Par 3
(183/160/152/145/111)

Speaking of quirky holes, the thirteenth certainly is that. How many par-3s feature pin positions that are out of sight from the tee? "Blind Man's Bluff" does, which puts a premium on your pin sheet and a good caddie. You'll need to have faith in both to have success on a hole inspired by Herb Kohler's visits to Ireland. In fact, Kohler specifically asked Dye to build a par-3 with a blind tee shot on his Irish course.

The hole features two completely separate teeing areas. One is immediately behind the twelfth green and high above the target. The black and blue tees are the only sets to see any action up here. From this position, the green sits in a hollow below mounds that completely obscure the target.

The second teeing area is down the hill to the left and at the same level as the green. From this position, you're able to see the left third of the putting surface. There is a lot of green hidden behind the mounds to the right that you can't see. In fact, this is a huge target at 14,000 square feet, with about 100 feet of green invisible from the tee.

The green slopes away on the left side, and a hump midway into the green shields the back left from view. If the pin is on the left side, that's not a bad place to be since you'll have an uphill putt. The thirteenth ranks as the easiest handicap hole on the back nine, but there are plenty of three-putts to be had here.

## No. 14 – Par 5
(564/520/508/469/380)

"Tullamore Dew" is another example of Dye tempting you into taking chances that don't necessarily improve your odds of success. Typically played into the wind, the fourteenth offers a good chance for par if played more conservatively than you may guess at first glance.

The tee shot must clear a large bunker that runs up the left side of the fairway, which angles from right to left. The more you try to cut off, the longer your carry needs to be. Assuming you're playing the correct set of tees for your ability level, the best line is at the trio of framing bunkers on the far side of the fairway.

The primary decision point is the second shot, which most players assume should be struck with a fairway wood to get as far down the hole as possible. That's not necessarily the wisest choice here. A creek crosses the fairway diagonally from left to right, ranging from 175 to 90 yards short of the green. Even for those who have enough length to clear the hazard, the resulting pitch shot from no man's land about 60 yards out is problematic.

The prudent play often is a layup down the right side to a position about 100 yards from the green. This largely takes the hazard out of play, since for most people it takes only a mid-iron to reach that point. Plus, this position is far enough back to put a full swing on your approach. The challenge comes in your distance control, as you will need to carry a cluster of bunkers that front the green from that angle.

Back right pin positions are the most difficult to access and carry the most risk. For bigger hitters, these pins offer a situation where carrying the creek on your second shot might make sense. The green opens from the left fairway angle, and the extra 15 yards of distance may create the space needed for a fuller swing.

## No. 15 – Par 4
(479/459/416/370/335)

This big hole, especially when played into the prevailing wind, is the No. 1 handicap hole on the course for a reason. "Frog Water" takes two mighty wallops to reach the long, narrow green, and par will earn a skin here more often than not.

Everything about this sweeping left-to-right design screams "stay left!" The fairway sits well above the rough and bunkers that populate the right side, and a creek and cart path play havoc with second shots that bounce down the hill short and right of the green.

Aim a little more left off the tee than your eye leads you to believe. It's a long way up to that point, and you'll want to be as far left as possible to set up the best angle to the green. Even if you won't be able to reach the green on your second, left is still the place to be for setting up your third shot. Bunkers pinch the back half of the green a little narrower.

Short and left of the green likely goes down a swale and into a catch basin, which is preferable to the trouble lurking to the right. Remember, bogey is not a bad score here. You're task is to take double bogey or worse out of play. Par is just a welcome bonus.

## No. 16 – Par 4
(474/436/425/383/333)

Things don't get much easier here, as Dye strung four of the five most difficult holes on the back nine for your finishing stretch. "Deep Dye" is a little easier than the fifteenth, thanks to the prevailing helping wind, but that benefit also can make approach shots more difficult for front pin positions. More on that in a minute.

Favor the right-center on the uphill tee shot to set up the best angle for your approach. Bigger hitters can catch a speed slot and roll out to within a short-iron of the green, and you will want to steer clear of the water that looms out of sight left of the fairway. Missing the fairway right sends you down a steep embankment, and it's impossible for all but the very long to carry the valley and bunkers at the elbow of the dogleg.

The approach is slightly downhill to a large, undulating and interesting green complex. Missing right is deadly, as a huge bunker awaits 20 feet below the surface of the green. Sand protects most shots from making it all the way to the water on the far left.

The prominent characteristic around the green is a pot bunker short and left. The slope off that bunker flows away from the fairway, making it difficult to hit it close to tucked pin positions. More green is available beyond and left of that bunker than it appears, especially when approaching from the left side of the fairway. The green accepts run-up shots right of the bunker, but be careful of running off the right side and down into the bunker of doom.

Big numbers definitely are available here, but par is not out of the question if you keep it in play.

## No. 17 – Par 4
(375/355/335/325/272)

There's no escaping the presence of water on "Irish Mist." A large irrigation pond forms the elbow of this sweeping dogleg left, and as the yardages indicate, length is not as important here as accuracy.

The landing zone is more generous than it appears, so feel free to err on the side of safety with something less than a driver. A silo in the distance is the suggested line, leaving an approach of 125-150 yards.

The wind direction is the biggest variable for the approach. The green sits hard against the pond on the left, and back pin positions require a full carry over the water. A south wind will test your meddle, as you may need to start your approach over the water and trust that it will bring it back to terra firma.

Dye generously leaves plenty of chipping space to the right of the green. A large bunker well right should not come into play. Despite the presence of water – and plenty of it – the seventeenth offers a good opportunity to score.

## No. 18 – Par 5
(558/536/523/493/388)

"Black and Tan" stands as the final example of Dye's three-shot hole design for par-5s so prevalent at the Irish. Remember after leaving the ninth hole when I suggested you take a glance at the eighteenth green on your way to the tenth tee? I hope you noticed that anything short of the green will funnel down a closely mowed hill away from the putting surface, leaving a very tricky pitch back up a steep hill to a blind green.

The best way for 99 percent of players to navigate this tricky finisher calls for a long-medium-medium approach to covering the distance. Here's what I mean:

The water feature you thought was in your rearview mirror when you left the seventeenth green is back to cause problems again on the eighteenth tee. The shoreline angles to the left, meaning you need more distance to carry the hazard the farther you take it to the left.

The suggested line is the mounded bunker formation that looks like a triangle at the far end of the landing area. Few can reach that bunker, especially when playing into the prevailing wind. That sets up a second shot, often with a mid-iron, to a spot beyond that bunker and short of a creek that crosses the fairway about 120 yards short of the green.

Have your caddie help you with the proper line here, because it's tricky. The safe zone is not large and not where you think it is. It's actually more to the left than it appears, and that area is blind from the tee shot landing area because of the downhill slope beyond the mounded bunker complex. Do not take aim at the green, because a layup will send you right of the fairway and into a rough area.

Now you're in position for a scoring shot up the hill, made a little easier by the fact you took notice of the green two hours earlier. Make sure to add a club or two to account for the steep change in elevation, and by all means, avoid the deep bunker left and below the level of the green.

The middle of the green is not a bad place to be in regulation while your playing partners struggle to get up and down. Win the match here and enjoy a black and tan back at The Irish Pub.

**Summary**

The Irish Course does not receive the publicity of its property mate, but don't let that deter you from enjoying one of the top fifty public courses in the country (according to *Golf Digest*). Many consider this track the more playable of the two, and thus, more fun. Take a caddie and you'll enjoy your round even more.

*Golf in Eastern Wisconsin*

# Blackwolf Run
# The River Course

## *Kohler, Wisconsin*

When Blackwolf Run opened in its original configuration 1988, course designer Pete Dye said, "There could not be a better natural setting for golf." The original eighteen holes have been split between the River and Meadow Valleys courses since then, but Dye's statement holds true today.

The River Course certainly lives up to its name, as the meandering Sheboygan River comes into play on virtually every hole. And where it doesn't, additional water hazards dot the ancient lake bed, including natural ponds and manmade irrigation ponds, and other soggy acreage.

Consistently ranked among the top public courses in the United States (No. 16 on the 2015 *Golf Digest* list as of this writing), the River Course offers a more traditional alternative to Kohler's Whistling Straits courses, but with enough brawn to host two U.S. Women's Opens. The USGA uses the original configuration for its Open setup, which includes holes 1-4 and 14-18 on the River Course. Spectator access to holes 5 through 13 would be too restricted by the confines of the river to make using the entire layout practical.

The River plays to a par 37-35 – 72, with the ninth green a long way from the clubhouse. The River Stand, a food and beverage building with restrooms, is accessible between the eighth green and ninth tee, and again after putting out on the twelfth green.

Walking is allowed at the River, with caddies available upon request.

**The River Course**
**Men's Yardages, Rating and Slope**
Black – 7,404 yards – 76.2/151
Blue – 6,865 yards – 73.7/144
Green – 6,507 yards – 72.1/139
White – 6,110 yards – 70.3/132
Red – 5,115 yards – 65.7/123

**Ladies' Yardages, Rating and Slope**
Green – 6,507 yards – 77.9/143
White – 6,110 yards – 75.7/138
Red – 5,115 yards – 70.3/125

**Hole Yardages (Black/Blue/Green/White/Red)**

## No. 1 – Par 5
(610/564/526/501/411)

    A strong par-5 to open the round, "Snake" demands a solid tee shot to avoid the Sheboygan River that bends in front of the tee and follows the hole up the left side the rest of the way. A lone bunker on the right side of the landing area stands as a solitary guardian for players who bail out away from the river. A series of mounds farther right are not a good place to be, but they are preferable to the river.

    The fairway bends to the right around a series of bunkers and small mounds about 150 yards from the green. The mounds aren't particularly high, but they're high enough to block your view of the fairway beyond. Take aim at the right side of the green, even if you can't get there, as that's the best line to set up your approach.

    The green is very deep at 48 yards long, with chipping areas to the right opposite sand and the river left. A valley that cuts through the putting surface about one-third of the way back creates significant challenges if you find yourself on the wrong side. Back left pin positions are the most difficult to access and bring more trouble into play.

    This hole may not seem quite so difficult if it came later in the round, but it presents a stern test right out of the gate. Par here will take a skin in many groups.

## No. 2 – Par 4
(377/370/355/345/310)

    Coming on the heels of a strong opening hole, "Burial Mounds" provides a brief respite as one of the least difficult holes on the front nine. The hole derives its name from the high mounds down the right side that separate it from the first hole.

    The fairway offsets slightly to the left from the tee, inviting a left-to-right shot shape. Large trees down the left side look troublesome, but there actually is more room down that side than it appears. Early morning shadows play with your depth perception and make the left side appear even more menacing than it is.

    There's no need to cut it close to the right side of the fairway, even if that may slightly shorten the hole. There is plenty of room left and you absolutely don't want to lose it into the mounds. Shots hit into the mounds are difficult to follow from the tee, which makes them challenging to find and leaves a blind shot to the green.

Many players swing something less than a driver due to the modest length of the hole and the desire to put the tee shot in play. An approach from the left side of the fairway provides a better view of the green, especially for pin placements on the right side behind a fronting bunker.

Be aware that the green slopes away off that front bunker and again in the back section. Long left is not a good place to miss because of long grass and a steep, uphill bank.

## No. 3 – Par 4
(468/410/395/389/295)

"Gotcha" comes at you next as the No. 1 handicap hole on the course. Often played into a quartering wind from the right, this dogleg-right hole requires a good tee shot to have any chance at par.

Take aim down the left side for the slightly uphill landing area, away from a deep bunker at the elbow of the dogleg that is certain bogey or worse. Mounding along the left side helps keep balls off the entrance road and in play.

Three large trees stand guard at the dogleg on top of the hill beyond the bunker. Their presence requires a sideways recovery back into play for any shot hit into that bunker. Even if you're able to skirt between the trees, chances are you will catch another bunker that runs up the fairway from that point all the way to the right side of the green.

The green is open in front to accept run-up shots and angles around the bunker to the right. The green slopes to the right, with a swale in the back left.

## No. 4 – Par 3
(219/195/185/146/117)

You may find your grip tighten a few notches upon arrival at this tee with the sight of "Swan Lake" hugging the right edge all the way.

Depending on pin position, this hole can play anywhere from a short to mid-iron thanks to the 42-yard-deep green. It helps to have a laser device in your group, since it's difficult to determine the pin depth from the tee.

Large mounds short and left hide the front-left corner of the green, as well as the presence of additional mounds and collection areas around the left side. The back-right portion of the green is narrower than the left.

No need to be a hero here. Just get on the dance floor and take your chances with the putter.

*The view from the fifth tee is heavenly at the River Course.
(Photo courtesy Kohler Co.)*

### No. 5 – Par 4
(427/400/388/376/275)

After driving up the hill to the fifth tee, park your cart and walk forward to reveal perhaps the prettiest hole on the River Course. "Oohs" and "wows" are common from first-time visitors as they look down on "Made in Heaven." Take a moment to admire the beauty of the hole, and then glance up at the green and make a mental note of the pin position. This is the last time you'll be able to see it until you arrive at the exceptionally elevated, table-top green.

The Sheboygan River frames the hole on the right, but far enough right to be out of play for all but the most severe slicers. Two large poplar trees guard the front left entrance to the fairway. They can come into play for players who favor that left-to-right shot shape.

The fairway angles slightly left to right, with a long, wide bunker down the right side about eight feet below the level of the fairway. That bunker gets a lot of traffic and usually necessitates a wasted stroke to get back into play. Another framing bunker on the left side of the fairway begins about 125 yards from the green. It is out of reach for many players, but longer hitters will need to steer clear of it.

Use an extra club or two on your approach to account for the change in elevation. The green sits well above the level of the fairway, with a hillside above on the left and a severe 25-foot dropoff to the right. The fairway runs up to the left side of the green, but it's all carry over the face of the dropoff from most positions in the fairway.

The tendency is to bail out left on the approach because missing right is so penal. However, a pitch shot off the hillside is very difficult because the green runs away from that direction. The middle of the green is a good spot for back and right pin positions, minimizing the risk of catching the dropoff and allowing for some release toward the hole.

### No. 6 – Par 4
(388/361/333/308/265)

"Jackknife" ranks as the easiest handicap hole on the front nine; that is, if you know where to aim your tee shot and which club to swing.

Assuming you are using a cart and won't hold anyone up, it's not a bad idea to drive ahead from the tee and take a look at the landing area. You need to aim more right than you would think; otherwise, a shot down what you believe to be the middle of the fairway can run out of room very quickly.

The hole bends rather sharply to the right around the river valley, which is out of sight behind the trees. The best line is just left of a large oak tree that stands at the right edge of the dogleg. You may need to play a fade even starting on that line, but be careful not to go too far right or you'll find the hazard. Most players go with a long iron or hybrid off the tee to set up a short-iron approach.

The fairway narrows as you approach the green, which shouldn't be an issue with the short iron you'll have in your hand. A bunker fronts the right portion of the green and the hazard hugs the right side. The putting surface is relatively small and angles from front left to back right. There is a little bit of room over the back left for chipping.

The hole should offer a good chance to score; however, I took an incorrect line off the tee on my last visit and made triple bogey. Just saying.

### No. 7 – Par 4
(426/401/374/352/293)

This dogleg-left hole is the mirror image of its neighbor, the sixth, only a little longer. From an elevated tee, the trouble is in front of you on "Glencary." A long, deep bunker that separates the two holes defines the left side of the fairway. A tee shot near that bunker provides the best line to the green, which angles from left to right.

It's possible to drive through the fairway, especially down the right side, so you may want to hit less than a driver. Longer hitters will have plenty of room from the back tees with a driver, and in fact, cutting the corner over the edge of the bunker with a driver is an option from more forward tees.

The ideal location for most players is 120-140 yards from the green, right where the fairway begins its turn to the left near the end of the bunker. A tee shot that finds the bunker leaves a blind second over mounds and more sand.

The challenging approach features a deep bunker left and short of the green, with a slope beyond that releases downhill to the green. Shots that land on that downslope will shoot forward and release to the right. Another deep bunker right of the green saves balls from continuing down the hill and into the hazard of the river valley.

Take extreme caution in firing at back-right pin positions. A miss to the right is automatic penalty with a kick into the hazard.

## No. 8 – Par 5
(532/524/492/470/401)

After a spectacular tee shot through a chute of trees and over a ravine, "Hell's Gate" swings around a hillside on the right and heads for a two-tiered finish.

The ravine requires a healthy carry to reach the fairway, which can be intimidating for players with lesser skill levels. Large trees that frame the left side of the ravine make it particularly difficult on left-to-right players.

Those with decent length can attack the dogleg, taking it just inside the tree line on the right. The hillside around the corner kicks forward toward the fairway and can trim significant yardage off the hole. However, long grass on that hillside can snare balls before they make it to the fairway, creating a very difficult stance if you're even able to find your ball. A bunker that frames the far side of the fairway is out of range for all but the very long.

The second shot presents an intriguing set of decisions, starting with the two-tiered, split fairway that defines the final 100-plus yards of the hole. The long, narrow green sets up best from the right, upper portion of the fairway. However, that target is tougher to hit than the lower portion of the fairway and brings the river valley hazard on the right into play.

The farther down the lower fairway you go, the more touch you need for your third shot. The green presents a very shallow target from that angle to an elevated putting surface largely out of view. As tempting as it may be to get as close to the green as possible, consider the savvy strategy of laying up slightly. It creates a little better angle to the green and offers the ability to impart more spin on the approach shot.

Long or right of the green is trouble, and left finds a difficult bunker well below the level of the green. A swale midway into the green on the left side collects a fair number of balls.

## No. 9 – Par 4
(361/337/316/302/238)

"Cathedral Spires" is one of Pete Dye's favorite holes because of the options it presents. In reality, this should be one of the easiest holes on the course as long as you don't get greedy.

The river on the right and an irrigation pond on the left should not come into play for most players. Towering cottonwood trees at the beginning of the fairway on the right side influence the tee shot, encouraging most players to hit left of them and away from the river.

Dye left a finger of fairway to the right of those trees on a direct line between the tee and the green. While that path certainly cuts distance off the hole, the risk of getting wet is way too high for ninety-nine percent of players. Seriously, don't let it tempt you.

The hole is short enough that you will have nothing more than a short iron in your hand when playing it safely left of the trees anyway. The green sets up for a better angle coming in from the left as well. The river is a concern only for far-right pin placements – or back pin placements when coming in from the left.

Use caution if attempting to fade a tee shot around the trees and toward the green. There is very little fairway there, and again, not worth the risk. Unseen from the tee, sand and grass bunkers comprise most of that area, leaving a more difficult lie than you would have only a few yards farther left.

Allow for some rollout on your approach, especially for front-left pin positions where the downhill slope will kick shots forward.

## No. 10 – Par 3
(227/204/194/175/147)

The first hole of the inward nine actually sends you to one of the farthest points from the clubhouse. "River and Marsh" is a strong par-3 that, as the name implies, sits between the river on the right and a marshy area on the left.

The green angles left to right, encouraging a matching shot shape. Make sure you swing enough club to carry the long bunker that runs up the right side between a collection pond and dry land. The river is further right, but certainly comes into play for overcooked fades.

Left and short is a good miss except for left-side pin positions. I've seen players unable to get within 10 feet of the hole from that position because of the significant slopes on that portion of the green.

Over the green and too far right are dead. The ideal target is smack dab in the middle of the green in most cases. Dye makes you choose your battles, and the back right of this green isn't one to pick.

## No. 11 – Par 5
(621/560/536/522/446)

"Rise and Fall" is a wonderful hole that will test your nerve and ability to execute under pressure, particularly on the second shot. More on that in a moment.

First, the tee shot must stay left of the river, which hugs the hole its entire length on the right. Longer hitters should consult their yardage guide to see if driver is the best choice here. The fairway narrows considerably at the far end of the landing area as the hole begins to turn right around the river. A bunker at the far end stops balls from reaching the irrigation pond beyond.

Here is where the real fun begins. The angle of the fairway makes it appear as though the best line for the second shot is over a bend in the river and toward the 100 yards of fairway short of the green – and it might be for bigger hitters. It also might be a dastardly trap set by Pete Dye to lure you into taking an unnecessary chance. Anything right finds the river and likely necessitates a drop all the way back from where you struck your second shot; in essence, a stroke-and-distance penalty.

A clump of four trees in the right rough around the corner stands about 150 yards from the green. Use that as your decision point when debating whether it's worth the gamble to bring the river into play. If not, there is plenty of room safely left of the trees, which still should leave a relatively short club into the green. The bunker on the left side of the fairway beyond those trees is about 90 yards from the green.

The putting surface is 37 yards deep, with the river crowding the back right portion and encouraging you to err left. Like most par-5s, the eleventh offers a legitimate chance at par or birdie. But if you're not careful, it can produce a big number, too.

## No. 12 – Par 4
(486/465/423/372/333)

The most difficult handicap hole on the back nine, "Long Lagoon" refers to the body of water players must carry off the tee to reach the fairway. The lagoon splits the fairway into two distinct halves. The right half requires much less carry to reach, while the left offers the best line to the green.

From the back sets of tees, the left half of the fairway is out of reach for all but the very long. Even from the middle (green) set of tees, it still takes a pretty solid poke of about 220 yards to clear the water and strip of sand that frames it. A pot bunker in the middle of the fairway ensures you don't have the entire width of the fairway to play with after clearing the water.

The Sheboygan River wraps around on the right to make its presence felt again on the approach. The long green wraps around a bend in the river, making the safe play toward the left side of the putting surface. The front of the green is open to allow long irons and hybrids to bounce onto the target.

Use the gigantic flag you can see off property on the hill behind the green to help judge the wind. This is a rather sheltered part of the course at ground level, and the wind can affect the ball's flight up high. Par will win the hole here more often than not.

## No. 13 – Par 3
(231/205/192/150/101)

It's not too often you need to carry a stand of mature trees to reach the green on a par-3, but that's the case at "Tall Timber," especially from the back sets of tees. A strong hole that can play even longer when the prevailing winds are up, this is an entirely different hole from the back tees compared to the forward tees.

From the back tee sets – which can include the middle green tees – the line is over the Sheboygan River and the edge of a stand of trees that obstructs the left half of the green. The river runs length-wise the entire distance before bending to the right around the side of the green. It's virtually all carry from the back tees.

The forward tee sets offset to the left of the trees, but still may require flirting with the edge of the branches depending on pin position. The green is huge at 53 yards in depth, with two bunkers left to capture those faint of heart with the river.

The front of the green slopes toward the river; the middle section leans toward the bunkers on the left; and the back portion is rather level. There is more room over the ridge that runs across the middle of the putting surface than you can see from the tee. Make sure to laser the distance to grab the right club.

## No. 14 – Par 4
(346/310/304/294/228)

The next two holes are the weakest on the course and provide a great opportunity to make up some ground. Standing on the tee at "Blind Alley," you can't help but think Pete Dye would have loved to have had more room to tack on some extra yardage. He didn't, so we get a reprieve from the strong string of holes that led off the inward nine.

Swan Lake borders the hole down the right side the entire way. The hole bends gently to the right, making the lake appear more visually intimidating from the tee. The strategy here is simple: Knock anything from a middle iron to a hybrid down the left-center of the fairway, and you'll have only a short iron in.

Be careful not to stray too far left, because and a large mound 75 yards from the green will block your view of the target. The mound narrows the fairway, and there's no need to risk hitting your tee shot that far anyway. You will want to stay well back from that point so you can put an aggressive swing on your approach shot.

The hazard hugs the green on the right, making the smart play no further right than the middle of the 40-yard-long putting surface. A bunker on the front left hides behind the mound from some angles, and the green slopes away off the bunker.

Can you imagine how much scarier this hole would be if Dye had an extra 100 yards at his disposal?

## No. 15 – Par 4
(374/354/346/329/290)

"The Sand Pit" isn't much longer than the previous hole, except without the fear factor of a water hazard. Instead, Dye uses enormous sand traps as the hazard of choice, and as the name implies, their depth certainly can cause a spot of bother.

The fairway angles from right to left, with a long, deep bunker defining the left side. The walls of the bunker are so steep that it requires a staircase to safely make the climb. The second shot is blind from down there, and another similarly large bunker lies in wait over the hill and only 50 yards beyond.

Remember the big flag referenced as an aiming point on the 12th hole? It's there for you again here. You can see it up on the hill from down in the bunker. Aim just right of that flag as a general guide.

*The par-4 fifteenth at the River Course (Photo courtesy Kohler Co.)*

A framing bunker on the right side of the landing area pinches the fairway at the crest of the hill about 100 yards from the green. Its high face blocks the view of the green from the right side of the fairway.

The best line off the tee is just left of that bunker with a 3-wood or hybrid, leaving a downhill shot of about 125 yards to a spacious green. Some players hit driver just inside the right bunker, but there really is little to be gained from that strategy. The fairway slopes downhill and toward the second bunker on the left, leaving you with an approach in the 75-yard, no-man's-land range.

A significant hump on the right side of the green can send approach shots on a wild kick. Other than that, the large green features a number of subtle undulations to make putting interesting.

**No. 16 – Par 5**
(620/560/540/511/483)

As you try and hold things together over the stretch run, the double-dogleg "Unter der Linden" presents a great risk/reward opportunity, especially for longer hitters.

The landing zone angles slightly toward left, bordered by a long bunker on the left that is well below the level of the fairway. While it is imperative to avoid that bunker, too far right isn't much better. A stand of trees on the right creates an elbow that blocks the fairway, limiting how far you will be able to hit your second shot. Sure, you can play a big left-to-right shot around those trees, but that requires starting the shot toward the Sheboygan River as it runs along the left side. The ideal line from the tee actually is as close to the bunker as you dare.

Bigger hitters may be able to reach the downhill slope past the bunker and roll out to a position that brings going for the green in two into consideration. That is no easy task, however. The shot likely will come off a downhill lie, with all carry required to clear a bend in the river that fronts the green.

A large linden tree stands sentinel at the edge of the river about 70 yards short of the green, taking away the option of playing toward the front edge. Tall, vertical railroad ties support the green on the opposite side of the river. It's quite the sight as you look down the hill.

The play for most is to hit the second shot as far down the right side of the fairway as possible. There is plenty of room right to bail out away from the river. If you're not able to get past the linden tree, make sure you're far enough right to hit over the tree or short enough to go left of it.

It's natural to give the river its due respect, but do not miss the green on the opposite side – over the green if hitting from a position short of the linden tree or right of the green if hitting from beyond the tree. A deep bunker awaits, and the last thing you want to do is blast out of that pit toward the river.

The green is very deep from right of the linden tree at 41 yards, and only moderately wide. Chances are you will have a downhill putt, since the green slopes toward the river. This is a super hole with lots of potential outcomes.

*The challenging approach to the par-5 sixteenth at the River Course (Photo courtesy Kohler Co.)*

## No. 17 – Par 3
(181/175/168/153/131)

"Snapping Turtle" is a strong par-3 that plays into the prevailing wind. A pond between the tee and green is home to a snapping turtle population – and more than a few golf balls.

The green angles from front right to back left, with the pond continuing along the left side. A series of grass bunkers on the right makes chipping a challenge for players who bail out away from the hazard.

The bank down to the pond is steep, leaving no room for error on shots that flirt with the edge. A lone pot bunker back right catches some shots hit too aggressively. That can be a good thing, though, since the Sheboygan River circles around the back of the green. There is a little room over the green, but not much.

The green is 43 yards deep, potentially creating a three- or four-club difference. The front half of the green slopes toward the pond and the back shelf is relatively flat. Make par here and prepare for the big finish.

## No. 18 – Par 4
(510/470/440/415/351)

"Dyehard" is a big hole that rewards length off the tee. Shorter hitters might have difficulty reaching this green in regulation, but Dye has left the approach open to accept running shots hit with longer clubs.

You may have seen this hole look a little differently on TV coverage of the two U.S. Women's Opens held here (1998 and 2012). That's because the waste bunker that defines the entire left side of the hole gets flooded for the tournament, creating a water hazard. Thankfully, that's not the case the rest of the time. The bunker still isn't a place you want to be, but at least it doesn't come with an automatic penalty stroke.

Playing your tee shot as close to the waste bunker as possible shortens the hole as it follows a gentle swing to the left, and a bunker on the right side keeps you honest. The right side of the fairway does have the benefit of opening up the approach to the green away from the big waste bunker.

The green sits in a beautiful amphitheater below the clubhouse and can feature swirling winds. Mounds and the hillside right of the green help kick wayward shots back toward the putting surface, which slopes to the left. The front-right portion of the green slopes away from the fairway and makes pitch shots from that position very difficult.

The green angles to the left and officially is 41 yards deep. Theoretically, you could find yourself putting from up to 100 yards away because of the double-green complex with No. 18 on the Meadow Valleys Course behind.

**Summary**

The combination of really difficult holes with relatively easy ones allows you to walk away from the River Course without feeling completely beat up. Play the correct set of tee markers for your ability level, and you will enjoy your trip around one of the USA's great public courses.

*Golf in Eastern Wisconsin*

# Blackwolf Run
# Meadow Valleys Course

*Kohler, Wisconsin*

It's pretty nice when all four courses in your collection rank among the best seventy-five public courses in the country. The Meadow Valleys Course at Blackwolf Run is an enjoyable trek over property alternately subtle and spectacular, as the name implies.

As you drive your cart over the Sheboygan River toward the starter's shack, take note of two things. First, glance to the left before you cross the river and check the pin placement on the eighteenth green. Not only will it assist with club selection later on, but it also will help you avoid a case of the shocks when you approach this target from the other side of the river.

Second, you will pass by an interesting-looking hole across the river on your right with no players on it. This par-4 was the tenth hole in Pete Dye's original Blackwolf Run design, but is not part of the current routing. The club maintains the hole for use in special events when the original routing is in play, such as the U.S. Women's Opens held here in 1998 and 2012. The green itself remains in use on top of the hill, only now it plays from a different angle on the plateau above as the tenth green of the Meadow Valleys.

The original routing featured holes 1-4 and 14-18 on the River Course as the front nine, and this now-unused hole and the current holes 11-18 on the Meadow Valleys Course as the back nine. The original tenth hole remained in play for several years until the expansion of Blackwolf Run.

Walking is allowed at the Meadow Valleys, with caddies available upon request.

**Meadow Valleys Course**
**Men's Yardages, Rating and Slope**
Black – 7,250 yards – 75.1/145
Blue – 6,830 yards – 73.2/139
Green – 6,450 yards – 71.5/136
White – 6,140 yards – 70.3/132
Red – 5,065 yards – 65.2/123

**Ladies' Yardages, Rating and Slope**
Green – 6,450 yards – 78.2/135
White – 6,140 yards – 76.4/131
Red – 5,065 yards – 70.4/118

**Hole Yardages (Black/Blue/Green/White/Red)**

## No. 1 – Par 4
(392/368/349/335/281)

Arguably the least difficult opening hole of all the Kohler properties, "Fishing Hole" offers an opportunity for a fast start out of the gate – that is, as long as your first-tee nerves don't produce a shot into the hazard on the right. That's easier said than done when you're amped up to play one of Pete Dye's gems, but the good news is there is plenty of room away from the pond on this short par-4.

The hole plays into the prevailing wind on top of the high ground that defines the Meadows portion of the course. Many players opt to swing a 3-wood rather than a driver to put the ball in play and set up a full swing for the approach. It's also possible to carry the hazard altogether as long as you have decent length.

The left side of the fairway provides the best angle into the green, which wraps around a bunker on the front right. From the tee, you may not see two flat bunkers that border the left side of the fairway. They begin roughly opposite the far end of the pond.

The green is fairly large for a short hole, with more room beyond the front right bunker than it appears. A small bunker also lurks out of sight behind the right-center portion of the green for those who give the front bunker too much respect.

Although the card lists this as the No. 7 handicap hole, it shouldn't be that difficult, and in fact this may be one of your best opportunities to score.

## No. 2 – Par 4
(402/392/385/375/278)

This interesting hole gradually ratchets up the difficulty factor with some of Pete Dye's trademark visual 'wow' factor. It's evident from the tee where "Table Top" gets its name, as the green immediately grabs your attention. While not long by any means, this hole earns its No. 5 handicap ranking by virtue of the severe penalty that comes if you miss the green that's perched high above the landing area.

The tee shot plays slightly downhill, with a line of trees on the right and three bunkers spaced along the left. The final bunker squeezes the fairway in half about 100 yards from the green, leaving the prudent play short of that spot. Allow for some rollout down the hill, and shots hit down the right side may kick toward the middle.

There's really no reason to attack this hole from the tee anyway, since you'll want to leave yourself a full swing on the approach to hold the shallow green. A sliver of fairway runs up the hill on the right side toward the green, but that's only useful if your tee shot finds the trees and you need to hit a runner from there.

The green is wide, with most of the putting surface accessible only by carrying the steep face that supports the target. Miss short or left and you'll have a virtually blind pitch up a 20-foot embankment. Anything long leaves a tricky pitch to a green that slopes away from you.

For a hole that shouldn't be more than a short iron in for most players, it still commands respect and is fun to play.

### No. 3 – Par 3
(182/176/158/142/110)

The easiest par-3 on the front nine hits out of a chute of trees to an open green complex. The target angles slightly left to right and is framed attractively by fescue-covered mounds.

"Pine Valley" plays with the prevailing wind, which you may not be able to feel from the sheltered tee. It's helpful to have a laser device in your group, with the 33-yard-deep green making correct club selection a necessity.

The primary visual hazard is on the right, where a rough area and bunkers sit below a shelf that defines the fairway short as well as the putting surface. While not an ideal place to miss, it doesn't necessarily spell doom.

Dye left several chipping areas around the rest of the green to make par saves a better possibility. Grab your par here and get ready to pull out the lumber on the next tee.

### No. 4 – Par 5
(565/539/516/473/428)

If you haven't hit a driver yet, which is possible, you'll be chomping at the bit to let one rip here. It's rare when Pete Dye sets up a hole that encourages you to blast away, but this is one of them. Go ahead and swing out of your shoes on "Gamble."

A huge bunker divides the fairway into two parts, with the left portion the wider and smarter option. It takes a very big hit to carry the bunker at its farthest point. Since the hole bends to the right around a bunkered hillside, the temptation is to cut off some distance by aiming for the right portion of the fairway. The recommendation here is don't fall for it.

The right portion of the fairway is thin, angled and difficult to hit. It doesn't even make a huge difference distance-wise. The right fairway option also robs you of the angle you need to access the green, assuming you have the length to get home in two. Dye placed some tricky mounds and a pot bunker out of sight immediately in front of the green from that angle, and anything right of that will find tall grass and potentially result in a lost ball.

Whether or not you have the length to go at this green, left is the place to be for several reasons: it's safer, you can see your targets, and the angles are better.

The conservative play on the second shot is a lay-up toward a bunker on the left that pinches the fairway about 115 yards short of the green. The more aggressive play is a 3-wood as far down the fairway as possible, setting up a short pitch to the smallest green on the course. Mounding left of the fairway helps keep wayward shots in play.

Big hitters can play a left-to-right shot into an opening on the left side of the green. The prevailing wind is from the left and often will assist in your shaping efforts. This is a good hole to play aggressively, as long as you're smart about it.

## No. 5 – Par 4
(403/380/362/340/314)

There are precious few trees on the Meadows portion of the course, but this is one hole where two particular stands of hardwood come into play. They form a chute into the green on the aptly named "Tree Stand."

The ideal line off the tee is over or just left of a series of bunkers that defines the right side of the fairway. The fairway angles left to right and offers more room down the left side, especially for shorter hitters. However, it is possible to run out of fairway on that line, and the left stand of trees will block your line to the green.

Approach shots from the far left side of the fairway or rough require a decision: play a right-to-left shot between the trees or bend a big left-to-right shape around the left stand of trees. The wind direction and your natural shot shape will dictate your decision, but keep in mind that missing the green left is dead if you are not fortunate enough to catch the large bunker there. There is much more room on the right from which to save par. In fact, the prudent play would be laying up into the fairway short of the green if you don't have a right-to-left shot in your bag.

The green is long and narrow, with correct club selection a critical component to putting yourself in position to score. Grab a par here while you can, because the next hole yields very few.

## No. 6 – Par 4
(475/470/444/406/341)

As if the raw yardage on "Serpentine" isn't enough challenge, this brute of a par-4 plays into the prevailing wind and is out of reach for many players in regulation. With that being the case, your strategy may be to play this as a three-shot hole, leaving par in play but removing double bogey or worse from the equation.

The view from the tee is visually deceiving. The front part of the fairway angles left to right and appears to bend to the left around a bunker that forms the elbow to the dogleg. It does dogleg left, but not where you think it does. What you can't see from the tee is a second bunker that lengthens the dogleg and makes it impossible to carry all the way to the fairway.

The best line is right of the bunkers, but as close to them as you dare. This line provides the best angle for your second shot as the fairway sweeps back to the right along the top of a sloping hillside. The route to the green down the right side features a series of small mounds, rough and a few bunkers thrown in for good measure.

A par here will feel like a birdie and win the hole in most groups. In fact, walking off with bogey is nothing to be ashamed of and is an even-money bet to win the hole.

## No. 7 – Par 5
(520/494/488/475/426)

This reachable par-5 ranks as the easiest handicap hole on the front nine. A welcome respite after the challenges of the previous hole, "Good Landing" nonetheless offers plenty of challenges that ensure this is no gimme par.

Typically played downwind, the slightly downhill tee shot should avoid the trio of framing bunkers that shape the landing area into a slightly right-to-left angle. The more left you go, the better the angle for the second shot. A pot bunker in the middle of the fairway about 150 yards from the green plays with your eye just enough if this is your second-shot landing area. Many players will clear this with little problem.

The real fun begins here, as a water hazard left and bunker right gradually squeeze the fairway as you approach the green. If you can't get all the way home, consider laying up to about 80 yards to take the dual hazards out of play and give yourself the biggest target.

From there, a wedge into the green gives you an opportunity score. Pin positions on the left side of the green bring the water into play. There is more green beyond the long bunker fronting the left side than it appears from the fairway.

There are ample chipping opportunities to the right of the green if you bail out away from the water; just take care not to go long or you'll find long grass atop the framing mounds that make recovery treacherous.

*The par-3 eighth at the Meadow Valleys Course is "Wet and Wild." (Photo courtesy Kohler Co.)*

### No. 8 – Par 3
(240/187/176/160/112)

How brave are you? Perhaps the better question is, how foolish are you?

Your tee set makes all the difference in how aggressively you can attack "Wet and Wild." Water is the primary visual element here, with a pond hugging the front and left sides of the green. A slight angle from the tee and a left-to-right prevailing wind in your face requires the tee shot to start out over the water on most days.

There is plenty of chipping space right and short-right of the green, so don't feel the need to be a hero if the situation doesn't require it. A large mound short and right of the green obscures that area, but take comfort in knowing you still have a shot at par as long as you find dry land.

The 37-yard-long green can play to widely varying yardages. Err on the side of taking the extra club here. A bunker behind the right-center of the green is the only issue with going long, while short is wet or stuck on the mound. Take disaster out of play and you'll walk away with bogey at worst.

## No. 9 – Par 4
(485/462/432/413/307)

Although the sixth hole ranks as the most difficult on the front nine, I'm not convinced this strong par-4 doesn't deserve that honor more. If nothing else, posting a big number here is more of a possibility, and that in itself makes "Deer Hunt" a test of skill and nerve.

The tee shot must carry a large, deep bunker that follows the fairway down the right side, at which point a water hazard takes you the rest of the way. The fairway angles left to right, and there is plenty of room down the left side off the tee. A safe line is just right of the large oak tree left of the fairway. Aim a little right of that if you have the length to comfortably carry the bunker at that angle.

The green opens from the left side of the fairway, and straight toward the green is really the only safe route. Bunkers guard the left side, while the pond sits tight on the right and wraps around the back of the green. Be careful to avoid a little piece of the pond that juts into the right side of the fairway just short of the green, too.

Par here is a very good score and gives you some momentum as you hit the halfway house. Grab a brat and get ready to take on the Valleys nine.

## No. 10 – Par 4
(382/366/330/320/242)

By far the tightest fairway on the course, this short par-4 is carved out of thick woods on top of the plateau above the Sheboygan River valley. It's not uncommon to see some wildlife while playing "Quiver."

Most players hit less than driver off the tee, where accuracy and careful placement are your goals rather than the length necessary over the previous few holes. The fairway doglegs right about 150 yards from the green. You can get a little closer to the target with a left-to-right shot, but beware of the pot bunker lurking at the corner.

The short- to mid-iron approach may feel the effects of the prevailing right-to-left wind, which you won't feel in the sheltered fairway. Left of the green is not a place you want to miss. One unfortunate kick is all it takes to send a wayward approach bouncing down the hillside.

The green is the smallest on the course and quite undulating. There is room for chipping among the mounds scattered beyond a small bunker right of the green. This shouldn't be a tremendously difficult hole, but certainly one where bogeys are plentiful if you miss in the wrong place.

*Missing the green creates challenges at the par-5 eleventh at the Meadow Valleys Course. (Photo courtesy Kohler Co.)*

### No. 11 – Par 5
(522/514/495/487/460)

    This fun hole offers a good opportunity to score prior to getting into the real meat of the Valleys nine. Often played into the wind, "High Country" is a reachable par-5 that invites big hitters to let out the shaft on the tee.

    An enormous, deep bunker defines the left side of the landing area as the fairway angles right to left. Pick out a line over the right edge of the bunker; anything left of that requires a big carry to reach the fairway. Finding the stairway-access bunker doesn't necessarily ruin your chances for scoring as long as you can make good contact down there. The fairway is blind from the bunker, but you'll put yourself in good position using the far point of the bunker as your target line.

    The fairway narrows as you approach the long green. The right rough drops down to a lower level that continues all the way to the green, where a large sand trap, grass bunkers and pot bunker all conspire to make getting up and down a challenge.

    Fescue-covered mounds left and behind the green provide help with depth perception, but they are no picnic to hit from. Allow for some rollout at the green, which slopes from front to back.

## No. 12 – Par 4
(461/438/407/395/327)

"Ledge Walk" ranks as the most difficult hole on the Valleys nine for good reason. This is a super hole that demands brawn and accuracy to walk away with par, coupled with the potential for big numbers if you're not careful.

The downhill tee shot sets up for a right-to-left draw off a bunker on the right side of the landing area. The prevailing wind helps here, and in fact it's possible to run through the fairway if you're a big hitter playing one of the forward sets of tees. That's because the fairway slopes down into a valley that cuts across the playing area about 110 yards from the green.

That brief break in the fairway gobbles up balls and results in a difficult downhill lie from rough for your next shot. If you find a fairway bunker off the tee or simply don't have the length to clear that valley on your second shot, you'll definitely want to consider laying up to the short grass in front of that zone.

The left side of the hole drops off into a ravine that plays as a lateral hazard. The ravine creeps more into play the closer you get to the green, culminating with disaster immediately left of the putting surface.

A collection area right of the green lies several feet below, making for difficult pitches to a putting surface that slopes toward the hazard. Par is well-earned here.

## No. 13 – Par 4
(341/335/313/304/233)

This short par-4 through the Weeden Creek valley will test your distance control on the approach. "Chimney" gets its name from the sharply elevated, tabletop green complex that features a blind putting surface from the fairway.

A fairway wood or hybrid is all you need off the tee to secure position for a short-iron second shot. The fairway swings to the left around a hillside with two large bunkers at the elbow. Even though the green is in line with those bunkers, the ideal line is just right of them to the fat of the fairway.

A laser device is useful in determining the correct yardage to the pin, since you won't be able to see the bottom of the flag. You'll want to add at least a half club to account for an uphill shot into the relatively long and narrow green. There is a small amount of sand to the right of the green, but most misses to that side disappear into the jungle.

Favor the left side of the green and you'll walk away with par more often than not.

*The par-4 fourteenth is one of the most dramatic holes at the Meadow Valleys Course. (Photo courtesy Kohler Co.)*

### No. 14 – Par 4
(423/409/384/376/293)

Simply a magnificent golf hole, "Nature's Course" very well could be the toughest par on the course, especially when the pin is toward the back of the 47-yard-long green. With trees and the Sheboygan River to the right and Weeden Creek coming into play midway into the hole on the left, trouble awaits seemingly everywhere.

The tee shot plays into the prevailing wind to a fairway that doglegs right. Take care to avoid driving through the fairway on the left and into Weeden Creek. Depending on conditions, the play here may be less than a driver.

The fairway offers more room down the left side and a better angle to the green, while taking it down the right side gets you closer to the target. Don't get too greedy trying to cut the corner, because tree branches will block your line to the green.

The hole begins its downhill trek toward the green about 120 yards out, with a gap between mowed sections at the steepest part. Should you find yourself in a position that calls for a layup second shot, your target is a small section of fairway about 60 yards short of the green.

Weeden Creek meanders around the green, creating a neck at the front, fanning out to leave room to miss on the left, and wrapping around to hug the putting surface along the back and right sides. Pete Dye's trademark railroad ties protect the acreage of the green complex from the creek the entire way around. It's truly an intimidating view from the top of the hill, and the wind can play havoc with your shot from the elevated fairway.

Needless to say, it's sheer foolishness to challenge any pin on the right half of the green. Play toward the left side and take your chances with the putter. It's not uncommon for bogey to win this hole.

**No. 15 – Par 3**
(227/196/189/150/103)

You'll want to take a look at this incredible par-3 from the championship tees even if you're not playing back there. "Mercy" definitely has the wow factor, because that's what you'll exclaim while looking at this jaw-dropping hole.

The massive green complex arises from the floor of Weeden Creek valley, with all carry required to reach safety. Anything short or left finds the valley and a likely lost ball. In addition to 48 yards of green front to back, there is plenty of room right and long for a wide safety zone. Take advantage of it, because the last thing you want to do is reload from the tee.

The green angles from front right to back left, with a significant swale running through the middle and back-center portion that collects a lot of shots. Chances are you're going to have a long first putt. Your task is to make sure your second putt isn't a long one, too.

**No. 16 – Par 5**
(590/544/487/478/415)

With significant differences in yardage and angles possible from the various tee sets, you'll need to consult your yardage guide to select the best line to this blind fairway. "Rolling Thunder" is a reachable par-5 for big hitters, but getting the uphill tee shot in play is requirement number one.

The fairway angles slightly left to right, with mounds guarding the left and a mowed rough area on the right well below the level of the fairway. A left-to-right shot shape works best as long as you don't overcook it. Should you find the right rough, the best line for your blind second shot is parallel to the fairway line next to you.

From the fairway, the downhill second shot invites you to go for the gold. The final 100 yards sweeps left to right around a massive, stairway-access bunker. Many a player has found that bunker, followed by multiple shots to extricate themselves. Getting greedy here is the fastest way to turn par into double bogey.

If you don't have the length to get home, play smart and give that bunker its due respect. There is room left or short to set up a short-iron approach. The best angle is from the left side of the fairway to the 43-yard-long green. Chipping areas on the left are benign, while shots over the green run down a steep embankment.

**No. 17 – Par 3**
(182/165/152/138/92)

Listed as the easiest handicap hole on the card, "Maple Syrup" offers a wide safety net right of the green that encourages you to err away from danger.

The long green is built into the hillside that slopes left down to the Sheboygan River valley. Anything short or left finds that valley and has a 50/50 chance of having a shot. A small bunker below the left side of the green saves a few balls from bouncing to their doom, but it's no picnic getting up and down from there, either. Bottom line: don't miss short or left.

The wind can increase the difficulty factor greatly, often blowing into you and from the right. An old maple tree, from which the hole gets its name, stands guard short and right of the green. With its base anchored below the level of the green, its height is not an issue for most shot trajectories. You will need to take your shot over that maple from all but the most forward tee position.

**No. 18 – Par 4**
(458/395/383/373/303)

You saw this incredible finishing hole when you crossed the bridge on your way to the first tee. Remember? At that time, you probably shook your head and wondered what that approach shot would be like when it counts. Well, you're about to find out.

The Sheboygan River comes into play on the right side of the landing area, and from here it's all carry to reach the huge double green shared with No. 18 on the River Course. More than a few approach shots find a watery grave on "Salmon Trap," where grips squeeze, swing tempos quicken and butts tighten with the stress of making clean contact.

A driver may be too much club off the tee, as a bunker at the end of the fairway guards an alternate green used by players using the red tees – or those unwilling to challenge the river carry. Right of that bunker gets you closer to the green, but also brings the river more into play. Note that the championship tee often plays from the primary teeing ground at 404 yards rather than from the 458 marker, which sits on a very small ledge halfway up the hill near the seventeenth green.

You will want to push your tee shot (or layup) as far down the fairway as possible to gain an open angle past the trees that guard the front right of the green. The putting surface is a whopping 63 yards deep, which explains the earlier suggestion to check out the pin position here on your way to the first tee.

Take plenty of club for your approach, since there is plenty of dry land long and lots of river short. Put a good swing on the ball and finish with a flourish. You might even get a little golf clap from the patrons watching from the clubhouse above.

**Summary**

The Meadow Valleys Course offers a nice mix of holes, both in terms of difficulty and topography variation. Often underappreciated because of its high-profile sister courses, the Meadow Valleys would be considered awesome if standing on its own merits. Make the effort to play here during your visit. You won't be disappointed.

*Golf in Eastern Wisconsin*

# The Bull
# at Pinehurst Farms

## *Sheboygan Falls, Wisconsin*

Situated on family-owned land only minutes west of Kohler's Blackwolf Run courses is Wisconsin's only Jack Nicklaus Signature Course, The Bull at Pinehurst Farms. The Bachmann family had operated a world-class Holstein breeding operation on this land for nearly a century before a series of devastating fires eventually launched a new dream for the property.

The Bull pays tribute to that legacy with each hole named for a bull bred by Pinehurst Farms. The golf course combines the natural beauty of the Onion River valley with the shot-making demands you would expect from a Nicklaus design to produce a truly enjoyable venue. Dave Bachmann Jr. runs the show, delivering a personal touch not always evident with national management firms.

"We felt we built the course on land that we had in our family, and that nobody could possibly have the same standards that we have in running it," Bachmann said.

"David Bachmann and his father worked very hard to allow us to do what we needed to do to produce a special product," Nicklaus said during a site visit prior to the course's 2003 opening. "They knew that in this area, they are competing against some very good golf courses, and they wanted to make sure they have something that can compete."

Nicklaus and his team successfully created a course that fit Bachmann's directive of "Challenge the best, and be fair to the rest." The golf industry agrees, with *Golf Digest* ranking The Bull No. 70 on its 2015 Top 100 Public Courses list.

"If I can get the women around the golf course in reasonable shape, I can generally get most anybody around," Nicklaus said of his philosophy.

The Bachmanns are well-acquainted with the concept of excellence. They had developed their Pinehurst Farms herd into one of the best in the world, becoming the first to earn Premier Breeder and Premier Exhibitor at all three national shows in the same year. They accomplished the feat twice, in 1976 and 1980. No other farm can make that claim.

A lightning strike in 1983 set fire to the main farm and destroyed the existing buildings. Fortunately, the cattle survived and the Bachmanns built a state-of-the-art facility that opened early the next year. But misfortune struck again in 1993 when fire again destroyed the milking barn. This time, David Bachmann Sr. moved the animals to another family-owned facility north of Sheboygan. The decision to move the herd freed up the Pinehurst Farms property for use in a new pursuit of excellence.

"I had always hoped to build a golf course, but having the barn fires gave us the opportunity," Bachmann Jr. said.

The first four holes sit on relatively open land that had been farm fields. Nicklaus said he is as proud of that stretch of holes as he is with the more visually dramatic parts of the course.

"Those first four holes, which we created out of absolutely zip, they look like some really nice golf holes to me," he said. "Then from the fifth hole on it's very natural, and it was just a matter of finding it. (Design coordinator) Chris Rule and David Bachmann found those holes. They spent a lot more time running through those woods than I did."

By the way, the land north of Sheboygan which became home to the Pinehurst Farms herd following the second fire also has a place in Sheboygan County golf history. The elder Bachmann eventually sold a farm at that location to Herb Kohler, who in turn traded the property to Wisconsin Power & Light. This transaction was necessary in order for Kohler to gain access to Wisconsin Power & Light property that he needed for developing the Whistling Straits courses.

As the late Paul Harvey would say, "And now you know the rest of the story."

**The Bull at Pinehurst Farms**
**Men's Yardages, Rating and Slope**
Bull – 7,354 yards – 76.3/147
Blue – 6,867 yards – 73.8/144
Green – 6,424 yards – 71.7/138
White – 6,027 yards – 70.1/135

**Ladies' Yardages, Rating and Slope**
Green – 6,424 yards – 78.0/146
White – 6,027 yards – 76.2/140
Red – 5,087 yards – 70.4/130

**Hole Yardages (Bull/Blue/Green/White/Red)**

**No. 1 – Par 4**
(424/412/365/344/281)

"Copyright" is a modest opener that still has enough kick to get your attention, especially if you have a tendency to hit your first tee shot of the day to the right.

Two bunkers on the right side of the landing area are the primary hazards to avoid off the tee, and there is plenty of room left to accomplish that task. With the green visible beyond the left edge of those bunkers from the tee, the temptation for bigger hitters may be to blast one over the left bunker and take a more direct line toward the target.

Don't do it. There is very little fairway on that line beyond the bunkers, and there certainly is little to be gained. In fact, that strategy brings into play the only real trouble on this hole, and that's the heavy rough and potential lost-ball territory right of the bunkers. The safer play is just right of a bunker visible down the left side. It's well out of range at only 60 yards from the green and provides a good visual.

The fairway slopes toward the green beginning about even with the right bunkers and the 150-yard plate, leaving a challenging downhill stance for your short-iron approach. You will need to carry the full distance to reach a relatively shallow green that sits back up the opposite hillside. A deep bunker fronts the right two-thirds of the green and makes your need to carry even more imperative.

A mowed area behind the center of the green collects approach shots that come in too hot, leaving a difficult, downhill recovery shot to test your mettle right out of the gates.

This shouldn't be an overly hard hole, but tricky putting and first-hole jitters on a great course often make par a winning score in your group.

## No. 2 – Par 4
(416/386/378/360/325)

Regardless of how you managed the first hole, "Blueprint" will elevate your heart rate as soon as you arrive at the tee. A large water hazard guarding the right side of this dogleg-right hole dominates the view, with the prevailing wind into you and from the left bringing the disaster zone even more into play on most days.

Nicklaus had little to work with in this part of the property in terms of interesting topography, so he created a large irrigation pond to spice up the action for the second and third holes. Mission accomplished.

The tee shot here requires carry to reach the fairway. It's up to you to determine how big of a bite you want to take off the dogleg. The penalty for finding water here is severe, because chances are you will not have crossed any dry land and will need to reload, hitting three. Nicklaus rewards players who go for a little gusto off the tee with a shorter second shot and a more favorable approach to the deep, angled green.

A large bunker frames the opposite side of the fairway in the landing area. Depending on your length and the wind conditions, the best line off the tee is a little right of that bunker. The 150-yard plate is even with the bunker as you face the green.

A bunker fronting the middle of the slightly elevated green removes most options for bouncing your approach onto the putting surface. There are a multitude of pin positions on this green, so make sure you check the GPS on your cart or your laser device to get an accurate yardage.

What this hole lacks in brute yardage, it certainly makes up for in the requirement for precision shot-making.

## No. 3 – Par 3
(216/194/184/169/120)

The par-3s at The Bull are strong in general, and "Peerless" certainly qualifies as a solid short hole. Played on the opposite side of the irrigation pond from the second hole, players with a tendency to hit shots to the right may begin to wonder when they'll catch a break.

Water dominates the right side again here, but there is plenty of room left and the prevailing winds push away from the water. Short left is the safe play, with lots of dry land and an opening into the long, narrow green encouraging this strategy.

Pin high and left can be problematic, however, especially if you miss the lone bunker guarding that side of the green. You likely will face a downhill pitch over that bunker. Depending on where you are in relation to the pin, it can be difficult to even stay on the green from that position.

A left-to-right shot shape works best with the angle of the green. Be sure to carry the large bunker fronting the right side of the putting surface, and of course, don't overcook the shot into the water.

A swale across the middle portion of the green makes the bulk of the putting surface invisible from the tee. Attacking pin positions in the narrow back portion is only for the truly brave (or foolish). There are times to play aggressively at The Bull, but this isn't one of them unless your skill set is quite high. The suggested play is to ignore the laser yardage when the pin is deep and simply play for the middle of the green.

While you watch your playing partners struggle to extricate themselves from trouble, you'll be glad you played for par.

## No. 4 – Par 5
(550/493/481/469/406)

Now here is a hole to consider playing aggressively – maybe. "Caravan" presents a great risk/reward design that offers equal opportunities for scoring and disaster. With the prevailing winds behind and from the right, this modest-length, dogleg-left hole sets up perfectly for taking a run at the green in two.

The tee shot is slightly uphill, with a bunker complex at the crest of the hill on the left and a bunker through the fairway on the right. In order to have a crack at reaching the green in two, you will need to carry those bunkers on the left. The danger comes in two forms: too far left and you bring out of bounds into play; too far right and it's possible to blow it through the fairway and into deep grass beyond.

The more aggressive your line to the left, the shorter your second shot will be. Plus, you will avoid a large tree that overhangs the fairway on the right about 130 yards from the green. Keep in mind that the farther left you take your tee shot, the longer of a carry you'll need to clear the triangular bunker complex. A good line for moderately long hitters is just left of the far-right bunker in that group. If you're successful in carrying the bunkers, your reward is a downhill kick off the back side and a helpful rollout to within middle-iron range of the green.

However, anything less than Position A off the tee leaves you with a decision: Should you go for the green, perhaps needing to bend one around that big tree on the right and bringing significant trouble into play near the green, or play safe?

My recommendation is to play safe unless you're highly confident in your ability to pull off a big shot. As tempting as it may be to try a hero shot when facing a yardage within your range, there's simply too much that can go wrong near the green. Deep bunkers in front and left of the green are worthy of respect, and you will need to carry the entire distance unless you're fortunate enough to find the slim opening on the left. Over the green brings a hazard into play as well.

Instead, swallow your pride and play for position. A large bunker 70 yards from the green on the right catches its share of "safe" shots, leaving an awkward distance that's too long for greenside sand technique. There is room in the fairway beyond that bunker and to the left, but that option leaves a 50-yard shot requiring a deft touch.

Staying short of the right-side bunker leaves a fuller swing from 80-100 yards. This is especially effective for pin positions in the front half of the green, where you'll need to put spin on the ball to keep it close. It's easy for approach shots lacking the necessary spin to release past the hole and down the hill toward the lower back half of the green, leaving a lengthy two-putt.

The wide range of strategy and scoring possibilities is what makes this hole fun. Anything from eagle to double bogey is legitimately in play. How aggressively do you want to play it?

*The fantastic fifth at The Bull at Pinehurst Farms*
*(Photo courtesy The Bull)*

**No. 5 – Par 4**
(436/404/388/361/308)

Growing up on the property, Dave Bachmann Jr. knew this hole was here when he took Nicklaus and his design team on its first walking tour. The team agreed as soon as they laid eyes on the treat that Mother Nature had waiting for them in the thick woods of Pinehurst Farms.

"This is one of my all-time favorite holes – anywhere," said Chris Cochran, Senior Design Associate for Nicklaus Design.

If The Bull has a "wow" hole, this is it. "Follow On" is a beautiful hole that tests your nerve and requires two quality shots to have a chance at par. Anything less and disaster looms on the No. 1 handicap hole on the card.

A deep ravine defines the hole in front of the tee and along the entire left side. There is some room in the right rough, with trees and thick undergrowth your penalty for bailing out too far. The fairway is generous, but that doesn't mean you won't be gripping a little tighter with the knowledge anything other than a straight, solid tee shot spells trouble.

Bigger hitters may want to pull something less than a driver here, as the fairway narrows considerably about 130 yards from the green. Too much distance down the right side off the tee risks running through the fairway as it begins its curve to the left around the ravine. Large trees that overhang short of the green on the right also come into play from that angle.

It helps to have a laser device with you, since this is a cart path-only hole and the GPS yardage on the cart will be of little benefit. Bring a few clubs out to your ball (along with divot mix) and err on the side of taking the longer club. The approach plays slightly uphill to a bowl-shaped green that sits on the opposite side of a bend in the ravine. Anything short or left is gone, leaving you to reload hitting four.

Once the fairway narrows, it remains little more than a sliver in width around the ravine all the way to the green. That means if your tee shot finds the right trees, your best play may be to position your second shot 130 yards from the green and take double-bogey out of the equation. There really is no good place to lay up the final 100 yards and it isn't worth the risk. If you can't reach the green, your assignment is to just make sure you have a third shot.

The front portion of the green slopes away from the fairway and hides most of the putting surface from view. It's natural (and advisable) to miss right or long if you're going to miss anywhere – and there is plenty of room to do so – but that leaves a downhill pitch to a green that slopes away from you.

Regardless of your score here, you'll find yourself looking back over the hole as you walk off the green saying, "Wow, that was an awesome hole."

## No. 6 – Par 3
(193/183/173/163/153 or 80)

This beautiful short hole plays downhill and requires all carry over a ravine to a long, two-tiered green. No pressure, but there's really no good place to miss on "Elation."

The front half of the green is the narrowest portion of the 38-yard-deep target, with bunkers guarding both sides. If you must pick a place to miss, beyond the right bunker is preferable to the hazard short and left. However, you likely will have a downhill chip to a green that runs away from you.

If you really bail out and hit one near the cart path in the trees to the right, your best option may be to pitch toward the back half of the green regardless of where the pin is located. It's virtually impossible to hold the front portion of the green from that angle, with sand and the ravine lurking beyond.

There is an alternate forward tee and drop area under the oak tree on the right, about 80 yards short of the green. If you have time while waiting on the tee, walk over to the far side and take a peek at the pin position on the adjacent green. That's the seventh hole, and you won't be able to see this from the fairway in a few minutes.

**No. 7 – Par 4**
(321/293/281/229/204)

    A quick glance at the distance may make you think you can get home with a good tee shot on "Starz." Maybe you can, but probably not.

    Minus an absolutely miraculous tee shot, all an aggressive play accomplishes here is bringing trouble into play. The elevated green sits well above a large sand trap that crosses the end of the fairway, while the Onion River makes its presence known to the right. A steep hillside left of the green and a putting surface that slopes away from the fairway make playing for position the wiser choice.

    The tee shot plays downhill from the back three sets of tees, with the widest portion of the fairway beginning over a marshy area 120 yards from the green. The savvy play is just short and left of a small bunker on the right that sits about 90 yards from the center of the green. This strategy takes the bunker out of play and provides enough approach yardage to impart some needed spin.

    Add a few yards to your approach calculation to account for the uphill, but keep in mind you will get significant rollout. The green slopes hard off the hillside from the left and away from the fairway. Accessing the back portion of the 41-yard-deep green requires taking a line along the left edge of the green. When in doubt, err left and let the hill kick your shot toward the green.

    There is some chipping room behind the green, with a bunker looming out of sight beyond the right-center. The amount of rollout makes it common for groups to arrive at the parking area behind the green and express surprise at where everyone's ball ended up.

    Putting requires some imagination to conjure up the correct line. Putts break sharply away from the hill, and uphill tries need a little more gas than you might think.

**No. 8 – Par 5**
(568/556/500/487/435)

    "Avant Garde" presents an interesting design concept that features two fairway options for the second shot. More on that in a second.

    Your choice of tee will play a role in determining how aggressively you can play this dogleg-right hole. For most players, this is a three-shot hole that plays into the prevailing wind and requires a bit of strategy to go with swing conviction.

    Big hitters can take it over the bunkers at the dogleg's elbow and create a chance at reaching the green in two. It's possible to drive through the fairway into the Onion River, especially from a forward tee area that chops at least 50 yards off the total distance. The landing area is wide if you're not trying to carry the bunkers. There also is a large safety zone in the left rough, well away from the lateral hazard that lines the right side.

Most players take their second shots up the right fairway, since it offers a shorter, direct route to the green and minimizes exposure to the river. The Onion River provides the dividing line in the split fairway, and there is carry required to reach the left fairway.

The left fairway comes into play most often for tee shots hit long and left. Go ahead and blast away if you choose the left option, because the farther you advance the ball down the fairway, the better your angle into the green. The left fairway is wider than it appears from the tee shot landing area.

When taking the more common right-fairway option, you'll give yourself the best chance at a successful lay-up if you commit to a specific distance and club. A shot of about 150 yards is all you really need to set up your approach. Too many players try to take something off a longer club and hit a poor-quality shot. Trees and the river come into play on both sides if you miss the fairway.

The green sits just over the river, presenting a wide, but fairly shallow target from the right fairway and a long, narrower target from the left fairway. A ridge divides the green in two, with a dastardly little grass bunker between the green and the river. Recovery shots from over the green are no picnic, but they're certainly a better option than finding the river.

## No. 9 – Par 4
(454/417/407/396/308)

For my money, this is the most difficult par on the front nine. Played uphill and into the prevailing wind, "Dynasty" can play considerably longer than its listed yardage.

Favor the left side off the tee, steering clear of a bunker and potential tree obstructions on the right. A long mound down the left side separates the ninth and tenth fairways. While it keeps wayward shots in play, getting stuck in the rough on the hillside creates a very awkward stance that usually eliminates any chance of reaching the green.

The Bull's impressive clubhouse stands watch above and behind the green, but what might catch your eye just as much is the deep bunker that guards the left front of the target. Between that bunker and the hazard to the left, you have every reason to bail out to the right.

The green angles from front right to back left, with a false front on the right requiring approach shots carry well onto the putting surface. Take at least one extra club to account for the strong uphill elevation change.

Back left pin positions are extremely difficult to access. In fact, the recommendation is to play for the middle of the green unless you have lots of game. Going after those pins brings the bunker and a hazard to the left more into play, and shots that miss pin-high right are dead on a hillside.

Par here will take a skin in your group more often than not.

*Don't miss right at the par-4 tenth at The Bull at Pinehurst Farms.*
*(Photo courtesy The Bull)*

### No. 10 – Par 4
(469/444/371/362/307)

A left-to-right shot shape works best on this hefty opener to the back nine, just so long as you don't overcook either of the two swings on the dogleg-right "Renaissance."

Typically played downwind, the elevated tee encourages you to let out the shaft and ride the jet stream. A pair of bunkers along the left side is ready to capture tee shots hit through the fairway. The bunkers make a good target if your length is more modest. Note that the middle (green) tees may be located on the elevated back teeing area rather than 70 yards forward at fairway level.

Bigger hitters can carry the large bunker at the elbow on the right, leaving a short to middle iron to the green. Be careful with this high-risk play, however, because anything in the bunker leaves no chance at reaching the green, and thick growth to the right of the bunker usually results in a lost ball.

A water hazard on the right begins 94 yards from the green. It acts like a magnet for layup shots, thanks to a fairway that slopes toward it.

The difficulty of the approach depends on the pin position and your length off the tee. The left side of the angled green opens to the fairway, accepting run-up shots that often follow the contour into the heart of the putting surface. A hillside left of the green and generous chipping areas on that side make this the preferred place to miss or even use as the primary target.

The right side is another matter. A long, deep bunker separates the green from the hazard below, and a small bunker behind the right-center of the target awaits shots that come in too hot. The green narrows as it moves right, creating a small target indeed for those skilled enough to take dead aim.

## No. 11 – Par 4
(353/331/320/309/267)

This short par-4 can be deceptive, especially when played into the prevailing wind. A large pond dominates "Medallian" its entire length, begging you to challenge it in the hope of increasing your chances at birdie. Little does the first-time visitor know that such foolishness only increases the chances of posting a big number.

Nicklaus presents two fairway options off the tee; one makes sense while the other is a sucker fairway more often than not. The primary fairway circles the pond around the left side and is the target for 99 percent of players, or at least it should be. Its generous width provides plenty of room to put a conservative tee shot in play and leave only a short iron to the green.

A bunker along the edge of the pond in the landing area seems like a good target to carry at first glance, but aiming left of that is the more prudent play. The fairway is at its widest left of the bunker, and the length of carry required over the pond and bunker can take you by surprise. Plus, successfully carrying the bunker leaves an awkward yardage for an approach shot that you'll want to spin.

The middle of the fairway left of the bunker leaves only about 100 yards to the green, and that's never a bad position. There is more room on that line than it appears from the tee, so don't be afraid to give it a little extra in case you push it right of your intended line.

A small bunker between the water's edge and the green is in play for many pin positions. The green slopes off the brow of the trap and away from the fairway, making it beneficial to leave enough yardage to spin your second shot. A 15-yard-deep chipping area behind the green gets lots of visitors and provides a decent opportunity to get up and down.

The other option off the tee involves taking it directly over the heart of the pond to an angled strand of fairway right of the green. While it's possible to carry the pond on a line right of the green, very few players have the length to actually reach the green. That's why it's a dubious strategy at best to take the right-side route. A long-hitting friend of mine came to this tee in contention on the last day of the Wisconsin State Open. He decided to go for the green in an attempt to make up some ground, dumped two in the water and walked away with an 8.

Play the hole conservatively and this becomes one of your best chances to score on the back nine. Take an aggressive route, and any number is in play.

## No. 12 – Par 3
(236/228/210/169/151)

"Primetime" is a big-boy par-3 that plays into the prevailing wind from the left. The elevated tee provides a spectacular view of what's in store for you, and there's a lot.

It's not often you discuss the benefits of hitting the fairway on a par-3, but this is one of those times. Since right of the green is dead, Nicklaus provided a generous bailout area short and left of a large green that steps off at 42 yards deep. Don't be afraid to use these areas to your advantage.

Setting up well left of the green to allow for the prevailing wind is a lot easier to execute when you see that nothing too severe can happen should your ball unexpectedly fly straight and true. There are bunkers scattered about, but finding one of them is preferable to the penalty shot likely with a miss too far right. A large bunker short and right of the green catches a lot of shots and saves balls from disappearing into the trouble right of the cart path.

The putting surface has many levels, with the left side offering an uphill putt to most other areas of the green. A par here will do very well in your group.

## No. 13 – Par 5
(581/564/523/509/425)

"Escapade" is a three-shot hole for all but the very long, thanks in part to a green complex that sits high above the level of the fairway. That's good news for medium hitters, since chances are you will be hitting your third shot from roughly the same yardage as your longer-hitting playing partners.

The prevailing wind from the right helps move tee shots into the heart of a fairway that angles to the left around a large bunker at the beginning of the landing area. If you have a right-to-left shot shape at your disposal, play this shot toward the bunker on the right and draw it in. A slight downslope will give you a little extra rollout, too.

Finding the fairway is crucial to setting up your second shot. The fairway rises beyond a series of cross bunkers between 200 and 170 yards from the green. Finding a bunker off the tee may limit your ability to clear those cross bunkers, effectively adding a shot to your journey.

The right side of the upper fairway beyond the cross bunkers is the ideal target for the second shot. There is plenty of room there, and that line will steer you well clear of two small bunkers about 100 yards from the green on the left. There's nothing more frustrating than attempting to play smart, only to find one of those bunkers and having to lay up from such a short distance. Trees on the left, the location of the green high atop a plateau, and a large bunker at the base of the hill conspire to make those little bunkers a bad place to be.

Leave yourself enough yardage for your third shot to put a full swing on the ball, because the green slopes steeply away from the fairway. You will want to create as much spin as possible while still allowing for some rollout. Hit enough club to account for the change in elevation, since you absolutely don't want to come up short of the hill's crest. It's to your benefit to hit past the hole and leave an uphill putt anyway.

There is a small amount of fairway on top of the hill in front of the putting surface, and about 20 yards of chipping area beyond the 42-yard-deep green. You won't be able to see the flag if your positioning shot advances too close to the hill that leads up to the green.

## No. 14 – Par 4
(475/436/396/382/293)

Your tee selection makes all the difference in the difficulty level of "Cornerstone." The blue tees, while not as far back as the 475-yard black (Bull) tees, often are offset to the right and present a difficult angle over the Onion River to the fairway. The forward tee sets are well ahead, in front a wetlands area, and offer a more direct visual line to the short grass.

The fairway doglegs right around a bend in the river, meaning anything right off the tee likely is wet. There is a little more room around the bend when hitting from the forward tee sets, but then trees can come into play. In fact, overhanging limbs can cause problems for approach shots hit from the right side of the fairway. The bottom line is, don't go right!

Two bunkers on the left frame the landing area, with the trap farthest out providing a good target from either of the back tee areas. From the forward tees, the bunkers still work well as a target if you play a left-to-right shot shape.

Your approach should favor the left side of the green, which opens to the fairway and accepts run-up shots. Play for some rollout here even if you land on the green. The putting surface slopes forward off the back of a bunker short left of the green, and away from a mound complex left of the putting surface. A deep bunker fronts the back right portion of the green and collects a lot of shots from its position in a low area.

There is ample room to play recovery shots around the green, but that doesn't mean they will be easy. Par here is always a good score.

## No. 15 – Par 3
(180/155/145/134/101)

This attractive little par-3 is the No. 18 handicap hole on the card. What "Landmark" lacks in distance, it makes up for with the heightened anxiety that comes with a water hazard definitely in play along the left side and in front of the angled green.

A generous cut of fairway short and right of the green offers sufficient bailout room, but the hole's modest length encourages most players to aim more aggressively than that. The danger ratchets up with pin placements in the back third of the green, which brings the water and a rear bunker into play.

The prevailing wind off the left may require a line that starts more over the water in order to hit one tight. Take care not to put too much stock in that wind, though. This is the lowest section of the course and somewhat sheltered from the wind.

Avoid an unnecessary mistake here, and get ready for an exciting trio of holes to finish.

## No. 16 – Par 4
(425/368/345/335/275)

When Nicklaus was working on the original routing for The Bull, he thought a hole in this part of the property would work best with a downhill second shot into the valley. There just was no way to make that routing work, however, and "Payday" ended up playing up out of the valley in the opposite direction of Jack's initial vision.

The result is a challenging hole that features a significantly uphill tee shot. While this may not be what Jack had in mind at first blush, the Golden Bear ended up with a very memorable hole that will test your skills.

Longer hitters likely need less than a driver here to ensure they don't drive through the fairway when it doglegs left on top of the hill. Anything through the fairway or even on the far side will have to contend with tall trees that encroach on the line of sight for the approach.

A bunker at the crest of the hill on the left is a good target if you can carry it. The ability to play a high right-to-left shape off the tee is big advantage, as a downhill slope beyond the bunker can propel balls to within a short iron of the green.

Players who shy away from the bunker and the trouble left will have a decision to make if they end up on the right side. In addition to the possibility of tree trouble, the distance required to carry the ravine in front of the green may be enough to encourage a lay-up. Allow for rollout if this is your option, since the fairway slopes toward the ravine that fronts the green, and you will run out of room about 50 yards out.

The green angles from right to left and is one of the more difficult targets on the course. It is two-tiered, with the back left portion higher than the front right. You must carry all the way to the green or the ravine – or if you're fortunate, bunkers fronting the left side – will be your demise.

There is room behind the green, save for a bunker long and left, but the only realistic place from which to get up and down is right. This position offers the best opportunity to pitch into the slope of the green. The transition between the two tiers is steep, making it imperative that you find the correct portion of the putting surface to have a chance at making a putt.

Despite its moderate handicap ranking, I would argue this hole is more difficult for higher handicappers than any par-4 on the back nine other than No. 18. More on the finale in a minute.

## No. 17 – Par 5
(572/541/525/484/416)

The final par-5 is one of my favorite holes on the course. A reachable par-5 when the wind is right, "Highlife" is a great risk/reward hole that demands decision-making regardless of whether or not you're going for the green. In either case, quality shots are a requirement.

Blast away off the tee to the most generous landing area on the property. The tee shot carries over a ravine and through an opening in the trees to find a fairway made even wider by the presence of a friendly hillside on the left.

Length is a definite advantage here. If you can reach a steep downhill that crosses the fairway about 230 yards from the green, the slope will propel your ball forward into a collection bowl and within consideration range of going for the green. The position high above the remainder of the hole provides an enticing view of what lies ahead.

Shorter hitters will have a decision to make for their second shot. The fairway ends about 180 yards from the green as the Onion River valley passes through. It picks up a wide 65 yards later on the lower level, 118 yards from the green. If in doubt, the smart play is a lay-up to the end of the upper fairway to set up a safer third shot.

The prevailing wind from the left can be helpful for shots from the upper fairway to the green. The putting surface presents as a wide, but shallow target from the top of the hill. There is an opening between a small bunker at the left edge of the green and a deep bunker in front.

Positioning can be tricky if you're not going for the green from long range. Bunkers either side of the fairway frame a last-minute dogleg to the right about 50 yards from the green. The left bunker is a better target, since it leaves an open fairway to the right and a more direct angle into the green. The putting surface is 33 paces deep from that angle, so you'll want to take note of the pin position to hit it close.

With the most difficult hole on the course waiting next, this is your last realistic chance to pick up a stroke.

*The strong finishing hole at The Bull at Pinehurst Farms*
*(Photo courtesy of The Bull)*

### No. 18 – Par 4
(485/462/432/365/312)

If ever there was a case to list a hole as par-4½, this is it. "Rock-N-Roll" plays into the prevailing wind and simply is a brute. Par here will feel like a birdie, and bogey isn't all that bad. Other than the eighteenth at Whistling Straits, this is one of the most difficult finishing holes you'll encounter.

The tee shot must carry a large pond to reach a fairway that angles right to left. The more you challenge the water, the better the angle and shorter the distance to the green. But bravery comes with a price, and in this case it's reloading to hit three if you fail to clear the hazard.

A pair of bunkers across the fairway awaits those who play it too safely. Just left of the second bunker is a good target if you have decent distance and the wind allows. The 200-yard plate from the green is roughly even with the leading edge of that bunker.

Shorter hitters will need to consider their options for the second shot, especially when playing into a strong headwind. A small creek that drains into the pond crosses the fairway about 150 yards from the green. The hazard area is about 35 yards wide, meaning you need to carry far enough to get within 115 yards of the green to find safety.

The creek and its accompanying wetlands follow up the right side the remainder of the hole, curving in front of and around the right side of the green. There are no sand traps near the green, but there doesn't need to be. With the hazard in front and a steep hillside behind, there is plenty of challenge when missing this target.

The good news about the hillside is it serves as no-doubt backstop to any shots going long. The bad news is the grass is thick enough to hold onto golf balls, leaving you with a very difficult pitch off a severe downslope to the green. That's still a better alternative than finding the hazard and likely a drop well back from the green.

The prudent play on days when even reaching the green is questionable is to play this hole as a par-5 and take your chances with the putter. The fairway is generous up the left side and the green opens from that angle. Bogey typically won't lose any ground in your group, and finishing with a smart play that limits the damage will send you to the clubhouse with a much better feeling than taking a big number.

**Summary**

The Bull at Pinehurst Farms is a low-key, family-run operation that fills a greens fee niche one step down from its higher-end neighbor without sacrificing the quality of golf experience. The enjoyable mix of holes on a fantastic piece of property makes this a must-play destination in Sheboygan County.

*Golf in Eastern Wisconsin*

# Erin Hills

## *Erin, Wisconsin*

The first couple of times I played Erin Hills not long after its initial opening in 2006, I came away with mixed feelings. Some awesome holes wound through the rolling Kettle Moraine region left by the receding glaciers ten thousand years ago, but there also were some downright goofy holes and green designs that had one of my playing partners swearing he'd never go back.

Erin Hills has changed since then, and most would agree for the better. The USGA requested changes in advance of the 2011 U.S. Amateur Championship and the 2017 U.S. Open Championship that included new holes, new or redesigned greens, and significant tree removal. The result, upon its reopening in 2010, is a fantastic layout that now deserves the description of masterpiece, as evidenced by its top-ten ranking among public courses in the U.S.

Located thirty-five miles northwest of downtown Milwaukee and about sixty miles southwest of Kohler, Erin Hills offers a golf experience unique to this region of the country. With its firm, primarily fescue fairways and natural mounding, Erin Hills conjures up images of the great courses of the Sandhills region of Nebraska and Northeastern Colorado rather than Wisconsin. Designers Michael Hurdzan, Dana Fry and Ron Whitten moved a relatively small amount of earth in sculpting Erin Hills. The team didn't so much design the course as discover it among the 652 acres it had at its disposal.

There is little ostentatious about the property. From the understated sign at the course entrance (which is easy to miss if you're not specifically looking for it) to the rustic look of the club's buildings, Erin Hills is golf for golf's sake. About the only building you'll see after leaving the first tee is the towering Basilica of Holy Hill east of the course.

The yardage from the back tees approaches the ridiculous at 7,812 yards, and believe it or not, Erin Hills can stretch even longer. Multiple tee boxes give tournament committees a variety of options for course setup depending on weather conditions and the ability of the field. Play a yardage to your handicap, even swallowing your pride to move up a set of tees. You will have all you can handle to post your average score wherever you play. Shorter hitters may want to consider playing the white/gold combination as marked on the scorecard, which at 5,585 yards is a full 600 yards shorter than the white tees. There also is a blue/green combination worth considering for stronger players.

Players can carry their own bag or hire one of Erin Hills' professional caddies. I strongly recommend going the caddie route to take advantage of their course knowledge and uncanny ability to locate wayward shots among the tall grasses and mounds that line the fairways. In addition, Erin Hills is not the easiest walk in the world. There are several uphill treks and a few long walks between holes. The caddies will enhance your enjoyment of what will be a special day of golf.

**Erin Hills**
**Men's Yardages, Rating and Slope**
Black – 7,812 yards – 77.9/145
Blue – 7,176 yards – 75.0/139
Blue/Green – 6,988 yards – 74.1/137
Green – 6,751 yards – 73.2/135
White – 6,228 yards – 70.5/129
White/Gold – 5,585 yards – 67.6/1234

**Ladies' Yardages, Rating and Slope**
White – 6,228 yards – 71.9/131
White/Gold – 5,585 yards – 71.9/124
Gold – 5,109 yards – 69.2/118

**Hole Yardages (Black/Blue/Green/White/Red)**

**No. 1 – Par 5**
(615/563/539/480/392)

The par-5s at Erin Hills are no pushovers, and this strong opening hole catches your attention right away with a lengthy carry to reach the fairway and a wetlands hazard to the left. There's no reason not to play it safe down the right side. A pair of bunkers on the right is out of range for most players, and the right side provides a better angle for your second shot.

A bunker on the left side about 185 yards from the green signals a dogleg left as the fairway moves uphill to a plateau. Another bunker frames the far end of the plateau on the right side about 75 yards from the green, at which point the fairway heads slightly downhill and again left toward the green. That means there is about 100 yards of fairway between those two bunkers, much more than it appears from the tee shot landing area.

Unless you have the power to go for the green in two, the recommended shot is a hybrid over the right edge of the 185-yard bunker and up onto the plateau. It may look as though you risk hitting through the fairway, but you have plenty of room. Your caddie will give you the line here, since anything left of that 185 bunker – or even directly over it from the right side of the fairway – brings the hazard down the left into play.

Allow for some rollout on your approach to a green that slopes away. With wetlands guarding the entire length of the hole on the left, err on the side of safety and you'll get your day off to a solid start.

## Hole 2 – Par 4
(363/341/322/322/231)

For a short hole, this quirky par-4 requires decent length off the tee to set up a good approach angle, especially when played into the prevailing west wind. The tee shot plays uphill, with the optimal line just left of the V formed by a large mound on the left in front of the tee and another mound across the fairway on the right. Your group's caddies will position themselves on top of the left mound to serve as forecaddies and point out your line to the blind fairway beyond.

The fairway angles right to left around the left mound and in front of a cluster of bunkers set into the hillside through the fairway. The hole swings back to the right beyond the bunkers, leaving a blind approach for tee shots that finish short or too far right of the visual opening.

Long and left off the tee is the only place you can see the green for your approach. This is a very difficult hole for short hitters, with about 200 yards needed to carry the left mound and reach the fairway. Players who are distance-challenged must hit toward the bunkers on the right to find the fairway, resulting in a blind second shot.

You'll chuckle when you hear this green was expanded from its original design. It's still a very narrow target and the smallest green on the course, and chipping is very difficult to the elevated putting surface. It's amazing how common double bogey is here despite its status as the shortest par-4 on the outward nine.

## Hole 3 – Par 4
(478/433/404/404/302)

Everything is visible from the tee on this straightaway hole. The downhill tee shot invites you to let out the shaft before heading uphill to a large green complex. Aim down the right side to take advantage of a landing area that slopes toward the left, taking care to avoid the bunker complex along the right. A second bunker complex on the left side of the fairway, a little farther out, is a magnet because of the fairway slope. You're still heading west into the prevailing wind, so consult your yardage guide to determine whether either of those bunker groups is within your reach.

A long bunker in the center of the fairway begins about 75 yards from the green and creates a subconscious distraction. The uphill slope heading toward the green tilts the bunker toward you and makes it appear as though the hazard extends all the way to the green. It does not. There is more room between the bunker and the green than it appears, so try not to let that affect your depth perception.

The green is large and features multiple levels. The transition between levels is much more severe on the right side, making it imperative you find the correct level for right-side pin positions. Any putts from the top level toward a bottom-right hole location will race right past. You actually have a better chance at saving par from short of the green than putting from the top shelf.

## No. 4 – Par 4
(439/439/398/385/283)

Huge bunkers in the middle of the fairway can play with your mind as they lead up the hill toward the green, but they are well out of range from the tee. Your only concern should be a bunker on the right side of the landing area that also is out of range for many players because you're still heading west into the prevailing wind.

The center bunker nearest the green absolutely does come into play on the approach, and more than a few players have taken multiple swings to extricate themselves. The approach shot is everything on this hole, with trouble in the form of a blind hazard immediately over the shallow green.

Unless you're highly skilled, the left side of the green should be your target regardless of the pin position. The green has twice the depth on that side, along with a hill behind the putting surface that serves as a backstop. Par here will win the hole more often than not.

## No. 5 – Par 4
(507/439/406/362/320)

Finally, it's time to head east and wrap up the last of a four-hole stretch of par-4s. A modest test from all but the way-back tees, the fifth is likely to play downwind more often than not. This hole offers a realistic opportunity to post a good score after the challenges of the opening quartet.

A small cluster of bunkers on the right side of the landing area is the only trouble on a very wide fairway. Reaching the left side of the fairway takes a little more carry over the long fescue, but this shouldn't be an issue except on the rare occasion of an easterly wind.

The short-iron approach offers an opportunity to be aggressive, with a bunker front left and two more back right guarding a large, mostly flat green. Be careful to avoid going long, as pitch shots from the framing mounds can be difficult.

The scorecard handicap rating might indicate that scratch players have a greater advantage over bogey shooters here than on the previous hole, but the prevailing downwind direction and generous targets actually make this hole much easier for players of average ability.

**No. 6 – Par 3**
(236/208/188/172/122)

The first par-3 on the course generally plays downwind, which makes holding the back half of the green that much more difficult. More on that in a moment.

The green is 47 yards deep, relatively narrow and angles slightly from left to right. Two design elements make this green particularly challenging: a false front your tee shot must carry; and the back half of the putting surface slopes away from the tee.

There is plenty of room around the target for chipping, especially over the green. A bunker right of the green makes the left side more attractive. Regardless of what your laser device tells you for back pin placements, take one club less and allow for some rollout.

This is a tricky little hole that nonetheless yields a healthy percentage of pars.

**No. 7 – Par 5**
(605/574/549/480/389)

This brute of a hole holds the No. 1 handicap on the card and is a stern test for most players. Played back into the prevailing wind and with a severe uphill finish, the seventh can provide a challenge to even get home in three shots. That is especially the case if you encounter any of the numerous bunkers that alternate sides of the fairway all the way to the green.

A tee shot down the left side is the preferred direction of attack, even better if you're able to execute it with length and a right-to-left shape. Big hitters can take advantage of a downhill rollout as the fairway turns slightly left around a trio of bunkers.

The second shot continues slightly downhill, with bunkers more prevalent down the right side than the left. The target is the left of two pot bunkers in the middle of the fairway about 80 yards short of the green. That line will steer you clear of bunkers on the right and set you up for a safe approach.

From a point short of those pot bunkers, the fairway rises steeply to a wide green that falls off significantly short right into a collection area. This is really a tricky little shot, with the surface of the green completely blind and often only the top of the flagstick visible.

Take plenty of club for your approach to counter the elevation change, and take into account the prevailing wind in your face that may not be as evident from the bottom of the hill. The collection area short right of the green gets a lot of visitors because of these factors. The putting surface is higher on the left side and falls away on the right.

While definitely a challenging hole and one that most players will not threaten in two shots, it still offers a reasonable chance at scoring despite its intimidating handicap rating.

**No. 8 – Par 4**
(490/439/411/359/250)

Your caddie may earn his tip on this hole alone, because without his guidance, you would have no way of knowing you shouldn't aim straight down the fairway. That's right, a tee shot straight down the middle can be trouble if you have any length at all.

A hillside left and a mature tree on the right make it appear as though the obvious line down the middle is the place to go. However, over the crest of the hill and out of sight from the tee, the eighth makes a hard left turn that sends unknowing tee shots through the fairway and into the fescue.

The line for many players actually is down the left rough line, or even left of that with a slight right-to-left shape. By this point in the round, your caddie will be able to advise you on the appropriate line and club (maybe a 3-wood) based on the wind and your ability level.

There are no level lies on this fairway. You likely will find yourself hitting from a downhill stance to an uphill green, fronted by three bunkers that catch a lot of shots. A backstop behind the relatively shallow green helps keep shots in play that come in hot from the downhill stance.

Par is a very good score here, but you stand a better chance with a caddie who can point you in the right direction.

## No. 9 – Par 3
(165/150/143/138/135)

What this hole lacks in distance, it makes up for with a demand on precision. This little beauty is no sure par if you miss the green. Played from atop the same hill that holds the eighth green, the prevailing right-to-left crosswind can make hitting the narrow target below far from automatic.

Back-right pin positions in the narrow neck are the most difficult to access, while the right-center of the green features a bowl that helps collect shots to that location. Bunkers virtually surround the green, with traps on the left significantly narrower and more difficult to escape with accuracy.

For a short, downhill par-3, the ninth is a stingier par than you might expect. Don't forget to grab your caddie a snack or refreshment at the halfway house behind the green while he heads in the opposite direction to act as a forecaddie on the next hole.

## No. 10 – Par 4
(504/476/450/427/298)

The back nine's opening test ranks as the most difficult par-4 on the course for average players, according to the handicap chart. At a robust 427 yards from the white tees, many players will find themselves negotiating this as a three-shot hole.

The fairway sets up slightly left to right from the tee, but be careful to avoid letting the prevailing wind from the left push your tee shot into trouble on the right. The ideal line to the blind landing area is just left of a bunker right of the fairway. Although it looks like a good idea to take it over that bunker, give it a little more respect to the left because anything right of the bunker's left edge flirts with disaster.

The good news is the fairway opens to a wide, welcoming carpet left of that bunker. Plus, many players can take advantage of a downhill slope over the hill that adds considerable distance to the drive. From there, it's uphill to wide but shallow green that's protected on the front right by a series of bunkers.

Bunkers left of the target serve primarily as a visual frame to the green complex. They are well left of the putting surface, with room in between for bailing out away from the right-side bunkers. The right side of the green is higher than the left, and a backstop there helps keep shots in play.

A par here is not impossible, but it certainly is well-earned.

## No. 11 – Par 4
(409/359/315/315/274)

Coming off one of the most difficult par-4s on the course, it's a relief to walk over to the tee of what may be least difficult par-4. At least that's the case as far as the handicap ratings are concerned.

The eleventh offers a chance to steady the ship after what may have been a rugged opener to the back nine. A short hole that features a wide fairway and little trouble to mar your journey, the eleventh may be just the ticket you need to post a good score. With that said, no championship course worth its salt will feature a gimme birdie hole, and Erin Hills is no exception.

The fairway offsets slightly to the right from the tee. The prevailing wind into you and from the right works with a fairway that slopes toward the left to keep balls in the short grass. The right side of the fairway offers a better angle into green, which slopes hard from the left.

Two large bunkers catch your eye at the far end of the landing area, but they are out of reach for many players. Consult your yardage guide to see if they're within your range. Whether they are or not, consider going with something less than a driver to leave a comfortable yardage for the approach.

The bunkers are well short of the green, especially the one on the left, so trust your laser device more than your eyes as you hit uphill into the green. The putting surface is oblong and deeper than it appears. Err on the side of missing right of the pin so you can putt uphill into one of the steeper grades on the course.

## No. 12 – Par 4
(466/432/388/388/317)

This strong hole plays into the prevailing wind and features one of the trickiest tee shots on the course. Your caddie will provide a major assist in helping with the line here as the fairway disappears to the right, around a hillside and down a slope.

If you're able to play a left-to-right shot off the tee, you can take advantage of the shape of the fairway to catch a speed slot that rolls down the hill and within a short iron of the green. That's a tall order, but the alternative is a longer, blind shot to a narrow green hidden by another hillside on the left.

The green you can see from the tee actually is the seventh green. Your destination won't become visible until you walk a few hundred yards. In fact, play this hole too far down the left side and you won't be able to see the green until you walk around that left hillside 75 yards short of the putting surface.

*The green at the par-4 twelfth at Erin Hills is hidden at the bottom of a winding valley. (Photo Mike Dauplaise)*

The suggested line from the tee is between a distant cart path and the right-most tree on top of the hill beyond the fairway. Take a chance at cutting the dogleg only if you can really pound it. A steep downhill about 170 yards from the green can help your ball release all the way to a flat area and a much shorter approach shot.

The lone bunker on this hole sits right of the green. It's okay to steer away from that bunker, because a slope coming off the hillside left of the green helps kick shots toward the putting surface. The slope creates the effect of having a more generous target away from the bunker. For back pin placements, keep in mind that the back third of the green slopes away. It's possible for balls to release all the way off the putting surface if you're a little too aggressive putting in that direction.

**No. 13 – Par 3**
(215/193/170/170/152)

This medium-length par-3 often plays shorter than its listed distance with the prevailing wind at your back. That's the good news. The not-so-good news is the helping wind makes it all that much tougher to hold a green that slopes away from the tee.

A pot bunker short left of the spacious green and a larger bunker beyond it catch a lot of shots. That's thanks to a swale running through the left side of the green that kicks balls toward those bunkers. A forced carry over a hazard from the tee, even from the forward sets, catches the attention of weaker players.

There is plenty of room to miss right and still save par. Really, anywhere other than left offers a decent chance at par on the No. 18 handicap hole on the course.

*The view from behind the par-5 fourteenth green at Erin Hills
(Photo Mike Dauplaise)*

### No. 14 – Par 5
(609/505/505/469/435)

      This is a good risk/reward hole, which means it has the potential for fun or despair. Depending on the wind, stronger players have a definite opportunity to reach this green in two shots. However, reaching the area around the green is no guarantee of birdie – or even par, for that matter.

      While it is debatable whether this hole truly qualifies as the most difficult on the back nine for average players, as the handicap chart suggests – or even the most difficult par-5 on the back nine – there certainly are enough challenges along the way to grab your attention.

      The tee shot must carry a set of cross bunkers in the landing area to have any chance at playing this hole aggressively. A tee shot down the middle of the initial portion of the fairway will run out of room and find the tall fescue on the right. The best line for longer hitters is toward the tree on top of the hill just left of the green. This opens the best angle to a blind fairway that lies down the slope beyond the cross bunkers.

      If playing this as a three-shot hole, your second shot should stay about 100 yards short of the green, where the fairway wraps to the right around tall grasses and the land of lost balls. Aggressive players will need to account for the extra distance needed to climb the 200-yard uphill stretch leading to the green. A laser device comes in handy here, as the direct line to the green often is shorter than the circuitous fairway route.

      For those going for the glory, the cart path visible on the hill behind the wide green is a good target. Do not miss right. In case you missed that, DO NOT miss right. The front-right portion of the green is a false front, sending balls bouncing down a steep hill toward possible doom. Pray for the bunker short right to catch your ball if it's heading in that direction.

The inverted triangle-shaped putting surface provides the strongest defense on this hole. It features two shelves, with the left side considerably higher than the right. Putts to the opposing shelf are extremely difficult. In fact, good luck even keeping your ball on the green if putting from the top shelf to the lower shelf when the greens are running fast. It can be that treacherous. A fun hole no matter how you attack it, the fourteenth has the potential to make or break your back nine.

## No. 15 – Par 4
(370/359/346/290/252)

As we head toward the farthest reaches of the property roughly a mile from the clubhouse, the short fifteenth is the last hole that plays into the prevailing wind.

The tee boxes sit immediately over the hill that frames the fourteenth green. There's nothing to block the wind that typically blows into you and from the left. The fairway below doglegs left and offers more room on the right than it seems. Even though playing down the right side of the fairway adds a little distance, it's still the best place to be. Small bunkers scattered diagonally across the fairway toward the right make the smart play something less than a driver for most players.

Keep in mind this is a short hole, so even a layup will leave you with nothing more than a shortish iron to the green. Too many players find a bunker or worse (the ball-eating fescue to the left) when trying to squeeze a tee shot into the small safe area over the first fairway bunker. It's just not worth the risk.

The uphill approach to a tabletop green requires an extra club or two to successfully make the climb into the wind. The left portion of the green has more depth when approached from the right side of the fairway; the right portion is deeper when approached from the left side. In either case, back-right pin positions deserve respect due to a narrow safety zone there.

## No. 16 – Par 3
(200/184/163/143/126)

This slightly uphill par-3 begins the prevailing downwind trek back toward the clubhouse. The primary challenge to this hole is an exceptionally narrow green that stretches 39 yards in depth. Use your laser device to get the correct yardage, since pin positions can make for multiple-club differences.

The green is fairly straight-on from the forward tees, but offsets increasingly as you move back on the tee boxes. A hillside on the left obscures the view of some pin positions, especially toward the back and left.

A backstop at the rear of the green helps keep balls in play on a two-tiered surface that slopes from back to front. With sand to either side, the only safe miss is a collection area short of the green and beyond a series of bunkers well short of the putting surface. Missing right offers a little easier recovery shot than from the left.

Grab your par here and prepare for more than a 1,000 yards of golf over the final two holes.

Yes, there is a fairway beyond this field of wildflowers on the par-4 seventeenth at Erin Hills. (Photo Mike Dauplaise)

### No. 17 – Par 4
(481/445/434/385/325)

As you make your way from the sixteenth green to the seventeenth tee, notice the way-back tee boxes available for tournament play. The one farthest back is more than 500 yards for this par-4. Hard to believe that's nothing more than a medium-iron approach for world-class players. But that's for those guys. Most of us will play distances here that are healthy enough without pushing the limits of reason.

The slightly uphill tee shot over a field of wildflowers is beautiful. One of the caddies in your group will go ahead to signal when the group in front clears the blind landing area. The right side of the generous fairway offers the best sight line into the green.

The green tucks slightly to the left at the end of the hole and hides behind a hillside short of the green down the left side. Tee shots down the right side have the best chance of seeing the pin on the approach shot, but even then, nothing is guaranteed. The rolling hills of the fairway can leave you in an area too low to see the pin.

There is more room left of the green than you can see from the fairway, while shots right of the green will find a collection area well below the putting surface. There is ample chipping room all around the green, and this is the only hole on the course without a single sand trap.

## No. 18 – Par 5
(660/637/620/539/506)

Welcome to what might be the longest finishing hole you'll ever play. For goodness sakes, this hole plays 620 yards from the *middle* tees! One of the caddies in our group got excited when he thought I had made a birdie after sticking an approach shot close. Unfortunately, I had to remind him about a short recovery shot I took out of a fairway bunker and that my shot into the green was my fourth.

"That's too bad," the caddie said. "If you had made birdie, it would've been only the second one I've seen here all season."

How often do you hear that said about a par 5? Not very often, which is what makes this finale so exceptional. Needless to say, it takes three solid shots to get home in regulation.

A set of framing bunkers on both sides of the landing area come into play from the back group of tees. Players hitting from the white tees, which sit 80 yards forward, may be able to carry those bunkers and bring into play a second set of bunkers that blocks the right side of the fairway.

Here's where the hole gets tricky. The fairway angles slightly to the right for the second shot and up an incline toward the next landing area. There is a cluster of bunkers on the left side about 160 yards from the green, at which point the fairway doglegs left around a sea of ball-devouring fescue.

A smaller bunker in the left-center of the fairway just beyond that cluster stares you in the face from its position on the steepest part of the hill. There is plenty of room right of that bunker and beyond it – plus, the fairway slopes right to left – so go ahead and blast away to take advantage of all that short grass up there. If you have the length to get up the hill, not only will you be closer to the green, you will have a much better view and angle to the pin.

Short and left is the only place you can't miss near the green. The round putting surface sits on a plateau exposed to the wind, with room to chip from anywhere other than left. Pars are possible here, but you'll certainly have to work hard to get yours. Chances are good you'll win the hole and smile a little wider during the stroll back to the clubhouse.

**Summary**

Erin Hills may not yet carry the big-name clout of Whistling Straits, but hosting major championships has a way of changing that. Erin Hills quickly has become a bucket-list course on the Eastern Wisconsin golf scene and definitely worth the short drive to discover this out-of-the-way treat.

*Golf in Eastern Wisconsin*

# The Bog

*Saukville, Wisconsin*

A half-hour drive south of the Kohler area brings you to the village of Saukville and The Bog, one of only two Arnold Palmer Signature courses in Wisconsin. As the name implies, the property features environmentally sensitive areas that add beauty as well as hazards to a course consistently ranked as one of the state's best since it opened in 1995.

The Palmer Course Design team moved relatively little earth in creating The Bog, but it did add significant drainage features and an extensive sand base to ensure a consistent bentgrass playing surface. The western boundary of the course abuts the Cedarburg Bog, a 1,700-acre feature that has been designated a National Natural Area Landmark, and 92 acres of wetlands are scattered throughout the layout.

"We didn't want to change the land that much, and we didn't have to because the property was so good," noted Harrison Minchew, formerly vice president and director of design for Arnold Palmer Course Design Co. "The Bog is as good as any course we've done. Fortunately, we didn't have to do that much to the place to make it a special golf course."

Course founder Terry Wakefield brought together 297 acres of land from three different families to develop The Bog. A reminder of the property's farming history remains to the left of the sixth fairway, where an abandoned barn stands sentinel at the dogleg of the No. 1 handicap hole on the course.

The Bog's greens are relatively quick, but the slopes are gentle.

"Arnold's philosophy is that if the green speeds are fast enough, you don't need to put a lot of contour into them," Minchew noted. "We don't like to trick up the greens."

One of the pleasures of good golf course design is using virtually every club in the bag, and The Bog has that feature. Employing an enjoyable mix of long and short holes for all three par types, The Bog keeps your mind in the game to the very end.

**The Bog**
**Men's Yardages, Rating and Slope**
Black – 7,221 yards – 75.3/143
Gold – 6,709 yards – 72.9/138
Green – 6,351 yards – 71.1/133
Blue – 5,911 yards – 69.1/131
White – 5,110 yards – 65.4/124

**Ladies' Yardages, Rating and Slope**
Green – 6,351 yards – 77.1/139
Blue – 5,911 yards – 74.7/133
White – 5,110 yards – 70.3/124

**Hole Yardages (Black/Gold/Green/Blue/White)**

**No. 1 – Par 5**
(530/491/471/427/401)

The opening hole eases you into the round with one of the best chances to score all day. A short par-5 with plenty of room off the tee, go ahead and blast away to see if you can put yourself in range to reach the green in two.

The tee shot plays uphill and into the prevailing wind, which can make the hole play a little longer some days. It's difficult to pick out the best line to the elevated fairway on your first visit. You can see a series of bunkers on both sides of the fairway, but the landing zone itself sits above the level of the tee boxes. The fairway offsets more from the left the farther back you go on the tees, and is a straighter shot as you move forward.

Since out of bounds looms left of the left bunkers, a good line is either at the inside edge of the left bunkers with a left-to-right shot shape, or just inside the right bunkers with a straighter line. Way right off the first tee won't kill you, but way left will.

The right side of the fairway provides the most direct line to the green and offers the best angle for your second shot. Bunker complexes begin pinching the fairway 88 yards from the green on the left and 68 yards short of the green on the right. The bunkers on the left end 44 yards short of the green, and it's downhill from there to a putting surface that continues sloping away.

That means if you're able to carry the right side of those left bunkers, you have a good chance of releasing all the way to the green and putting for an opening eagle. Keep that slope in mind if you're coming in with a shorter iron for your third shot, too, and allow for some release. There is plenty of chipping room short and left, away from bunkers that guard the right side and behind the green.

## No. 2 – Par 4
(396/372/358/330/282)

Check your math on the tee here to make sure you're not using too much club. The fairway ends about 100 yards from the green, and the modest hole length gives you the flexibility to go with something less than a driver and still have a comfortable distance to the green.

Unlike the first tee, this time the fairway offsets more to the left as you move forward on the tee blocks. The view is straighter from the back tees.

A pair of bunkers frame the left side of the landing zone, potentially saving errant shots from the out of bounds immediately left of them. However, playing too conservatively to the right can leave you with an obstructed view of the green and no good place to lay up. A valley between the end of the fairway and just short of the green features rough-level grass that you certainly can play from, but then you're dealing with unpredictability and lack of spin for your shot into an elevated green.

The green angles from the front left to behind a series of bunkers set below the level of the putting surface. Short left and pin-high left are the safest places to miss. Long is OK, but leaves a difficult downhill pitch from the second cut.

Play this hole strategically and you should have a good opportunity to score.

## No. 3 – Par 4
(424/398/358/338/271)

Your length off the tee makes all the difference in the suggested line here. Your ability to carry a set of cross bunkers at the elbow of the slight dogleg-left determines whether you can take a more direct route to the green. Do the math from your tee of choice and make sure you can carry to a point 140 yards from the green or less.

Especially when played into the prevailing wind, you will need a solid strike to carry the bunkers and reach the generous landing area beyond. Your reward is a short-iron approach with a favorable angle into the green. There is no guarantee you will be able to advance the ball far enough to reach the green should you find the bunkers.

Taking the less-aggressive route around the cross bunkers adds some distance to the approach, but still leaves only a middle iron into the green. The

150-yard mark is between the cross bunkers and a pair of bunkers that frame the right side of the fairway. The right-side bunkers are a little farther out from the tee and will be out of range for many players.

Up at the green, a long bunker on the left side protects balls from bouncing out of bounds, while a collection of bunkers on the right protects pin positions on that side of the green, particularly when approaching from the right side of the fairway. A chipping area behind the green provides a reasonable opportunity to get up and down.

## No. 4 – Par 3
(210/196/184/171/144)

The first feature to catch your eye upon arriving at this difficult par-3 is the large expanse of bunkers fronting the angled green. This sea of sand features five traps that force a carry to virtually every section of the green, except for the very front left from the forward tees.

A left-to-right shot shape works best, but you must strike it with precision. The dreaded straight shot can send your ball bounding down an embankment and into the junk left of the green. Overcooking your fade to the right of the bunkers leaves a very difficult up and down, but at least you'll be able to find your ball. There is a chipping area beyond the bunkers and to the right of the rear section of the 39-yard-deep green.

Catching the sand is preferable to going long on most occasions. There is little to stop a ball from reaching trouble behind the green during the firm conditions of summer. A par is a well-earned score here.

## No. 5 – Par 4
(469/422/393/379/330)

A substantial carry over a wetlands area makes it imperative that you put a decent strike on your tee shot. The ideal line can be difficult to determine from the tee, but a good target is just left of two trees you can see through the fairway along the right side. The trees themselves are out of reach for most players, but they can interfere with approach shots coming from the right rough.

A long bunker down the left side of the landing area and a small bunker in the right rough shape the serpentine fairway. There is room in the rough short of the right bunker, which is a preferable miss compared to left of the fairway. The landing zone begins to pinch at the right bunker about 180 yards from the green, with its narrowest point coming 125 yards out, roughly even with the two target trees.

The green is open in front and on the right side, with bunkers left and long. Putting yourself in position for a clear second shot is the key to scoring on this hole. Accomplish that, and your chances for making par are pretty good.

*The par-4 fifth at The Bog requires accuracy off the tee.*
*(Photo courtesy The Bog)*

## No. 6 – Par 4
(415/415/395/372/280)

The No. 1 handicap hole on the course also is the most unique, with an abandoned barn contributing to a dogleg on the left side of the landing area. The fairway curves around a bunker in the left rough and the unusual barn visual to find a relatively small safe zone.

The tee shot must traverse a significant natural area to reach the short grass, and a large triple tree at the end of the fairway on the right can block approach shots from that direction. The ideal line off the tee hugs the left side of the fairway. A right-to-left shot shape comes in handy to follow the shape of the fairway.

The trees on the right combine with an unmowed valley that crosses the fairway 100 yards from the green to create a dicey decision for the second shot. Do you simply pitch out to a spot short of the valley and take your chances with a wedge third shot? Or do you challenge the hazard down the left side and try to cut one around the trees and reach the green? That's a high-risk option, since anything left of the green is dead. There are chipping areas available to the right of the green.

You will need two quality shots here not only to score, but in some cases to avoid disaster.

## No. 7 – Par 4
(449/409/398/367/334)

A bog passes in front of the tee and continues behind the trees that line the left side, encouraging a line down the right side of this slight dogleg-left hole. Tee shots have a substantial carry to reach the fairway, which then opens to a generous landing area devoid of bunkers.

Challenging the left side of the fairway offers a better angle into the green, and a mound that is more prominent down the right side can put the brakes on your rollout. A pair of bunkers guards short and right of the green, which is a common miss because of the hazard to the left.

The green is narrow and relatively deep at 34 yards, with a closely mown chipping area over the back. There is plenty of room right and long to bail out away from the hazard.

## No. 8 – Par 3
(220/188/170/150/138)

Arguably the strongest par-3 on the course (No. 13 may take exception to that claim, but more on that later), this brute plays into the prevailing wind and is all carry over the bog. This certainly is a big boy hole from the back tees.

Two rows of tee sets provide alternate angles into a large green guarded by bunkers to the left and red hazard stakes tight on the right. The middle of the green is never a bad place to be on this hole. Take your par and happily move on to the ninth tee.

## No. 9 – Par 5
(543/521/493/467/401)

This is a three-shot hole for most players despite its moderate length and downwind tendency. That's because the penalty for missing the green can be severe, even if you have a chance at reaching the target in two.

Multiple tee sets create opportunities for the grounds crew to alter the angle to the fairway, particularly from the back tees. Generally speaking, the best line from the tee is a little left of a water tower visible on the distant hill. The fairway offsets from the right, with a bunker field below the level of the fairway on the left that forms a slight dogleg.

A favorable wind and a big hit make it possible to carry the right edge of the bunkers and roll out to within the decision zone of going for the green.

A mature tree left of the fairway is 226 yards from the green, and it's all downhill from there.

The fairway widens to create a generous lay-up zone from about 100 yards to 60 yards short of the green. At the 60-yard mark, the fairway angles left around a pair of bunkers and through a very narrow opening. A hazard on the left encroaches short of the green and wraps around the left side, with several bunkers waiting to grab balls hit to the right.

The front portion of the green continues the narrow trend and slopes away from the fairway. You have a better chance at drawing a reasonable chipping opportunity long and right than long and left.

Cross the entrance road immediately behind the green to access the halfway house and the tenth tee.

## No. 10 – Par 4
(410/399/381/353/307)

You can't see much of this hole from the tee, as the fairway heads uphill to a ridge and then downhill all the way to the green. The portion of the fairway that's visible invites tee shots on a line more to the right than is necessary. There appears to be acres of short grass to the right, but that's not the case for most players.

While there is ample fairway at the crest of the hill, most players can drive past this point and release down the hill. Tee shots hit down the right side soon will run out of fairway, making the optimal target closer to the left rough line. The target line is a little right of that from the back and forward tees, both of which are offset to the right.

The fairway widens a little over the hill down the left side, and a speed slot there can propel balls to within a short iron of the green. A lone bunker is out of sight over the ridge on the left, but it's a little more left of where you would think the fairway is and within range of carrying it with a solid shot anyway.

The green is 40 yards deep, narrow in the front, and open for approach shots coming in from the left. A large bunker short and right of the green is the only major trouble and forces a carry from the right side of the fairway. This is a good opportunity to get your inward nine off to a good start.

## No. 11 – Par 3
(152/142/132/121/100)

The No. 18 handicap hole on the card is short and sweet, but the Palmer Design team created plenty of opportunities to find trouble.

Played slightly uphill and into a prevailing wind from the right, it's important to find the correct portion of the narrow, two-tiered green. You may need an extra club or two to account for the elevation change and any hurting wind.

The green slopes hard from the right, making a downhill shot from either of the two bunkers guarding that side a challenge indeed. Another bunker short and left sits well below the level of the green, but offers a generally easier uphill shot to the putting surface as long as your ball doesn't finish too close to the steep face.

*The shallow target at the short, par-4 twelfth at The Bog*
*(Photo courtesy The Bog)*

### No. 12 – Par 4
(348/318/306/279/239)

Now here is an interesting little par-4 that invites aggressive play but rewards patience. There are pros and cons to both.

The fairway doglegs right around a pair of bunkers and two clumps of trees 120 yards from the green. A long series of bunkers frame the left side until about 100 yards from the green.

While it may seem the obvious play to blast a tee shot over the dogleg and within a flip wedge of the green, that strategy may not be the most prudent option. Trees begin to encroach on the line of flight as you approach the green, making shots that find the rough on either side a candidate for being blocked. A rock-lined creek in front of the green takes away the option of punching a run-up shot under the branches.

In addition to the potential pitfalls of hitting a long tee shot off target, successfully pulling off that shot leaves its own set of challenges. The green is extremely shallow, especially on the right side, and a 50-yard approach shot over a creek is a difficult distance to dial in, much less create spin. There are chipping areas over the green, but that is no automatic up-and-down.

Taking the fairway bunkers out of play is the primary benefit of playing aggressively off the tee. The more conservative play invites a narrower landing area, but a fuller swing for the approach. Either way, this little devil will have you shaking your head if you fail to execute.

"The twelfth was really just a natural hole," Minchew said. "We cut the bunkers into the hillside just as a guide, then filled in the green and put a wall in front of it. It's neat when the shortest hole on the course is one of the toughest."

*Anything not on the green likely is in trouble at the par-3 thirteenth at The Bog. (Photo courtesy The Bog)*

### No. 13 – Par 3
(195/175/157/142/110)

The most picturesque hole on the property is a great par-3 that demands nerves of steel to find safety.

The tee shot is all carry over a ravine and a long bunker that leads up to the green. A few more bunkers wrap around the left side and frame the rear section of the putting surface, which angles from right to left and follows the contour of the ravine.

There is a small chipping area for those who bail out right, but only for the front portion of the green. Trees and very rough terrain come into play beyond that, and shots to back pin positions that miss pin high to the right will find trouble.

Be prepared to yell "fore" for tee shots headed right. The fourteenth tee and cart path are immediately right of the thirteenth green. It's so close you might think the group ahead forgot to move their carts out of the way after putting out.

Despite the rather benign handicap ranking of 16, par here is always a welcome score.

## No. 14 – Par 5
(528/498/476/440/390)

Without previous course experience (or reading this book), there's no way to know your chances for making birdie here actually decrease by playing the hole as it is designed compared to taking a short cut only the regulars know exists. More on that shortly ...

The downhill tee shot heads into a wide landing area bordered by a hillside on the left and thick woods on the right. Check your yardage guide for the distance to the end of the fairway on the right, because it is possible to drive through at that point.

At the far end of the landing area, approximately 225 yards from the green, the fairway squeezes through a very narrow opening between the hillside left and the woods right before opening up again about 100 yards from the green. The fairway then bends to the left and uphill all the way to the green, with two large cross bunkers menacing your approach 50 yards short of the target.

The dogleg left around the hillside and a stand of trees on the corner make it extremely unlikely to reach the green in two when taking this route. Here's where the locals' secret short cut comes into play. Rather than hitting the tee shot down the right side toward the fairway opening between the hillside and the woods, the locals take it down the left side toward what looks to be jail, blocked by the steep hillside.

However, players with decent length know they can take their second shot up over the hill, between a gap in the trees, and with a little left-to-right shape they'll find the blind fairway beyond. The shot requires the ability to get the ball up quickly – and this strategy isn't for every level of player – but if you've got the game to give it a try, go for it. Just make sure to send a playing partner up the right side first to ensure the landing area is clear before giving it a rip. The fairway widens substantially immediately past the crest of the hill.

This route not only shaves considerable distance off the hole, it also takes the cross bunkers out of play. Even if you come up short of the green, the left portion of the fairway is at a level similar to that of the green and offers an open view to the pin.

There is ample chipping room around the green, making this a fun, multi-option hole to do a little gambling.

## No. 15 – Par 4
(470/433/412/402/341)

This strong par-4 plays to a relatively narrow fairway which angles slightly to the right. The elevated fairway can make it a little difficult to determine the best line off the tee, but a building behind and left of the green makes a good target.

A series of mounds in the rough down the often-visited right side of the landing area can create challenging stances as you play through a chute of trees about 100 yards short of the green. Often played into a quartering wind from the right, it takes two solid shots to reach the slightly elevated target. A sidewall right of the green helps keep wayward approach shots in play, and there are plenty of closely mown areas for chipping.

This is one of those holes where big numbers are rare, but par will win the hole more often than not.

## No. 16 – Par 4
(439/398/367/336/311)

The sixteenth has a handicap ranking slightly easier than the previous hole, likely due to the shorter distance, but many players will find this hole the bigger challenge. That's because unless you have a right-to-left shot shape in your arsenal, this dogleg-left tester effectively becomes a long hole that features one of the more difficult approach shots on the course.

Situated at the far reaches of the property, the fairway doglegs 80 degrees around a pond and wooded area before heading uphill to a green complex partially hidden by a field of bunkers. A strong hook (for right-handers) puts you in position for a medium-iron approach. Minus that shot, the higher-risk option calls for a high tee shot over the trees on the corner to a blind target. Anything less than perfect on that line often results in a lost ball. The farther left you go, the longer the carry that's required to reach safety.

The bunker field short of the green can be deceiving. The leading edge is 86 yards from the middle of the green, with a narrow ribbon of fairway around to the left. There is plenty of room between the final bunker in the series and the putting surface, so trust your yardage more than your eye.

The green is fairly deep and angles left to right. Short and left is the preferred place to miss due to significant slopes from the back and right sides. Par is a good score on a hole where strokes can pile up quickly.

## No. 17 – Par 5
(593/520/520/474/419)

There's a lot going on with the top-ranked handicap hole on the back nine as we make the turn for home. The first suggestion is to ignore your primal instinct to automatically reach for the driver on any par-5. You may need it, but for most players, this is a position hole in which placement trumps distance.

The tee shot landing area wraps around a hazard from right to left. Having the ability to shape your shot to match the design again offers a distinct advantage, since it's possible to run out of fairway fairly quickly down the right side. You're better off keeping your ball back in the fairway a bit than pushing it to the far end, since trees there can obstruct the view of the second-shot landing area.

A 65-yard gap in the fairway over a hazard area begins a long uphill stretch toward the green. A lone tree in the left-center of the fairway, 153 yards from the green, narrows the effective opening even more.

The ideal target zone for the second shot is 90-100 yards from the green, just before the fairway begins to pinch. A clump of trees on the right and a string of bunkers in front and up the left side come into play 74 yards from the middle of the green. There is a slice of angled fairway beyond the first pair of bunkers and in front of a pair right of the green, but you invite trouble by trying to inch your way closer when it may not provide much benefit.

Keep in mind that if you're able to advance your tee shot around the corner to very end of the fairway, you still have 240 yards uphill to reach the green. If that's more than you have in your bag, laying up short of the trouble likely will save you more strokes than you would gain attempting to push it as far up the fairway as possible.

## No. 18 – Par 4
(430/414/380/363/312)

The home hole is a good one, providing a worthy test to conclude the day. Ranked as the most difficult par-4 on the back nine, there is plenty to absorb visually from your vantage point on the multiple elevated tee sites layered into the hillside.

For the first time in several holes, a left-to-right shot shape comes in handy off the tee. The fairway bends to the right around the largest water hazard on the property, with mature trees lining the inside of the dogleg between the pond and the cart path. Bigger hitters may want to take it over the edge of the trees, but take care not to bite off too much – the tree line extends down the right side and the fairway ends 119 yards from the green anyway.

With that being said, driver may not be the play for everyone. Bunkers down the left side of the fairway frame the landing area opposite the pond, and it's possible to drive through the fairway and into them, especially with the prevailing wind blowing from right to left. The far end of the last bunker is 151 yards from the green, making 3-wood off the tee an option worth considering.

A 50-yard gap in the fairway brings you to a small patch of fairway for those unable to get all the way to the green. A long bunker guards the left side of the putting surface, which features a significant hog's back midway into the green on the right side.

Keep your ball in play here, and par will send you to the clubhouse for a post-match beverage in a little better mood and possibly with the final skin of the day.

**Summary**

The Bog is a quality layout that can challenge any skill level as long as you play the appropriate tees. Open approaches to many of the greens make the course playable for lower skill levels, but there are enough forced carries around the property to make it a big test for very short hitters. Use discretion in picking your spots to play aggressively and you will navigate the course more successfully than most.

*Golf in Eastern Wisconsin*

# Brown County
# Golf Course

*Oneida, Wisconsin*

My definition of a good design is being able to play a golf course over and over without getting tired of it. That's the case with this classic Larry Packard design from the late 1950s. Brown County, or "The County" as the members refer to it, has been my home course since 1989.

While not in the elite company of other courses featured in this book, many consider Brown County the best public course in Northeastern Wisconsin. *Golf Digest* ranked Brown County among the top fifty public courses in the country prior to the high-end course construction boom of the 1980s.

Set in rolling hills and woods of the Oneida Tribe of Indians' reservation, this affordable, county-owned layout is only an hour north of Kohler and ten minutes from the Green Bay area's major tourist attraction, Lambeau Field and the Green Bay Packers. There are no roads, housing developments or any other signs of civilization around the property; just a tranquil, relaxing vibe enhanced by incredible natural beauty. This parkland course is traditional golf at its best, with Packard's design leveraging the terrain without forcing the issue.

"I had a chance to pick from two or three other sites closer to town, but this one was by far the best," Packard told me in a 1991 interview. "It has been a fantastic thing as far as I'm concerned. I definitely consider it one of the top courses we've ever done."

Brown County struggled mightily for decades with poa annua greens that often failed to make it through the winter. Finally, with the course's loan for a new clubhouse paid off, the county board approved the investment necessary to completely renovate the greens in 2013.

The result is pristine, bentgrass putting surfaces with improved drainage and new bluegrass chipping areas. Brown County is back in business as one of the region's elite courses, and members who endured months of temporary greens are delighted with their new playground.

You'll want to make hay while the sun shines on The County's first few holes. (That's Midwest-speak for "take advantage of a good situation while you can.") Many a player has coasted through the opening trio of holes with visions of a career round in the making only to come crashing back to earth when the course bares its teeth beginning with the difficult par-4 fourth.

Pin colors are red, white and blue from front to back on the greens, and red maples on each side of the fairway provide visual approximations for 150 yards from the green.

**Brown County Golf Course**
**Men's Yardages, Rating and Slope**
Blue – 6,749 yards – 72.1/133
White – 6,392 yards – 70.7/128
Gold – 5,954 yards – 68.7/125

**Ladies' Yardage, Rating and Slope**
Red – 5,675 yards – 72.6/1272

**Hole Yardages (Blue/White/Gold/Red)**

**No. 1 – Par 4**
(370/354/341/338)

The opener at Brown County is one of those holes that eases you into your round and seems ripe for a fast start. After all, how difficult can a relatively short par-4 with no real trouble be? But the members will tell you that birdie wins a skin here more often than not.

The hole turns slightly left against a gentle slope that tilts to the right, making it a difficult fairway to hit for players with a typical left-to-right shot shape. A lone framing bunker on the left side of the fairway also encourages shots a little more right, although many players can carry that bunker without a problem.

Mature trees down the right side are set back from the fairway far enough to leave room for error. Left is another story, however. Anything left of the bunker is trouble, encouraging a subconscious bailout to the right with the first swing of the day.

The downhill approach reveals a round green guarded only by a large bunker that sits well left of the putting surface and doesn't get much play. The open front allows shots to bounce onto the green, but beware of rolling through because a chip from over the back is tricky.

Pin positions across the back are the most difficult to putt, and the general slope of the green toward the right is more pronounced than it appears thanks to Trout Creek passing by the neighboring seventeenth green. The first is an "easy" hole, yet one the members are still pleased to walk away from with a par.

**No. 2 – Par 5**
(498/459/421/351)

The tee shot is one of the more stressful ones of the day, especially from the blue tee, and the early-morning sun can be blinding during the middle of summer.

This short par-5 (par-4 for women off the forward tees) plays longer than listed because of a hill at the far end of the landing area. Still, longer hitters can reach the green in two without much problem, particularly from the white tee. It's not uncommon to see a backup on the second tee as players wait for the green to clear before hitting their second shots.

The hill crosses the fairway about 200 yards from the green and acts like a wall, keeping otherwise well-struck tee shots from rolling out. The result is a blind second shot that requires a playing partner atop the hill to give the all-clear signal.

Despite its propensity for giving up birdies, the second also produces its share of disasters. There is little room for error off the tee. Trout Creek makes a zigzag path across the fairway, with more distance needed to carry the hazard down the right side than down the middle.

Don't get too carried away favoring the left side, though. The stream makes a right turn in the woods left of the hole and swings back into play, with a bend appearing smack dab in the landing zone in the left rough. After a penalty drop, overhanging branches restrict the shot choice to nothing more than a punch up the fairway. Before you know it, you're facing a long fourth shot to a tough green to hold and damage control is in full force.

Favor the left side of the fairway for your second shot to take advantage of an opening to the shallow green. A large sand trap guards the right two-thirds of the green and catches a lot of balls, while a smaller trap farther left grabs those who give the fronting bunker a little too much respect. Another bunker looms over the green and down an embankment to save overaggressive shots from continuing into the fourth hole behind.

The green slopes slightly away beyond the front bunker in the front, requiring a deft touch with spin to get close to tight pin positions. Savvy players will lay back far enough to put a bigger swing on their approach and impart the needed spin rather than attempt an awkward pitch over the bunker from 40 yards. The bunker laughs at those who get too cute with that pitch.

## No. 3 – Par 3
(157/133/124/121)

The easiest hole on the course offers a good chance at par or birdie before entering the meat of the layout. From the white tee, the hole plays slightly uphill to a rather large, bowl-contoured green. The elevation is about even from the blue tee.

A bunker left of the green catches pulled shots, but it's a better alternative than missing the green right and watching your ball kick into thick bushes. Err toward the fat of the green for any right-side pin placements for just that reason.

Be cautious about going after back pin positions too aggressively. The rear portions of the green slope noticeably from back to front, increasing in severity as you move toward the left side. It's very difficult to keep chips near the hole from over the green.

The grounds crew typically places the gold tee blocks on an alternate area left of the primary tee. This brings the left-hand bunker more into play, especially for left-side pin positions.

## No. 4 – Par 4
(423/414/395/337)

The No. 1 handicap hole on the card interestingly is the only hole on the course without a sand trap. That doesn't mean disaster isn't lurking on this strong, tree-lined par-4. While not overly long by modern standards, this dogleg-left hole still packs a punch for most players, especially when it plays into the prevailing wind.

The primary challenge comes off the tee, where players need to find the relatively small window available for an open shot to the green. Too far left and trees will block your path if you're fortunate enough to stay out of Duck Creek; too far right and trees that come into play 100 yards off the tee can play pinball with errant shots, usually dropping them too far back to have a go at the green.

It's also possible for longer hitters to drive through the fairway and find themselves blocked by trees on the far side. If you want to try cutting the corner, you'll need to have enough length to get within about 140 yards of the green. Short of that and you will find yourself at least partially blocked. Just a little bit of a tug left and Duck Creek comes into play, and double bogey or worse will be your fate. A shot into the hazard produces a drop that leaves nothing more than a punch out to the fairway.

Despite the added length in playing down the right side, members will take that option any time compared with missing left. Carry the initial stand of trees on the right and there is a clearing beyond.

There's nothing particularly tricky about the approach shot other than the tree-lined beauty of the Duck Creek valley. The easiest chips come from short or left of the green. The green slopes from front to back and right to left. Local knowledge says putts tend to go a little more toward the left side of the green than they appear, particularly from the center of the green and left.

**No. 5 – Par 4**
(362/348/333/331)

This short par-4 plays a little longer than listed with an uphill tee shot into the prevailing wind. The ability to play a right-to-left shot off the tee is a big advantage on this dogleg-left hole. The angle of the tee sets becomes increasingly difficult as you move back, with the blue tees predictably presenting the most difficult angle.

Slicers (at least the right-handed variety) have a difficult time with this tee shot. Trouble looms left in the form of a bunker at the corner and a line of thick vegetation that typically results in a lost ball. Shots that tail right often go bounding away from the target, leaving a second shot that's either blocked by trees or too long to reach the green (or both).

Bigger hitters can take it over the right side of a fairway bunker to cut off some distance and leave only a short-iron approach. There is a little more room beyond the leading edge of the bushes to the left of the bunker than it appears, but be careful not to cut it too close, because shots have a tendency to kick left there.

A tee shot to the top of the hill leaves a short- to mid-iron approach to a relatively flat green guarded on both sides by bunkers. The left side of the green slopes toward the middle, making par saves from the left bunker less likely when short-sided. Restroom facilities and vending machines are located behind the green.

**Members' tip:** As you walk up the fifth fairway after hitting your tee shot, take a glance to the left and check out the pin position on the neighboring thirteenth green. It may affect your club choice when you get to that tee. More about that later.

*The uphill approach to the par-5 sixth at Brown County
(Photo Mike Dauplaise)*

**No. 6 – Par 5**
(524/511/473/414)

This dramatic par-5 tests your ability to hit from uneven stances and shape your shots. The fairway is virtually impossible to hit unless you're blessed with exceptional length. The first 250 yards slant severely toward the Trout Creek valley on the right, typically leaving a second shot from the rough and the ball below your feet.

The creek is well right of the fairway, but it does come into play, particularly during the dry season when the grass isn't thick enough to stop shots from rolling to a watery grave. Doubling the penalty is the fact the fairway doglegs right around trees, meaning you can't do much more than punch your third shot back into play a short distance down the fairway.

There is a flat zone on the far left side of the fairway, but anything pulled left finds a row of thick trees and bushes, often resulting in an unplayable lie and/or a punch out. If you're fortunate enough to keep it in the fairway there, and you find a spot the members refer to as "the launching pad." This little area offers a straight view down the fairway from an elevated position.

The common play is to aim down the middle off the tee and watch helplessly as the ball bounces into the right rough. Take your medicine, play a little cut shot around the corner of the dogleg and into position for a short- to mid-iron third. Big hitters can fly it far enough to reach a downhill slope and roll out to within range of reaching the green in two.

The hazard follows the hole on the right the final 150 yards, only this time with the fairway slanting away from it to the left. With the ball typically above your feet for the third shot, it's easy to pull your approach toward a large bunker on the left or over the shallow left portion of the green. The uphill approach makes depth perception difficult. The green is a little deeper on the right side.

Putts on the right half of the green break toward the left more than they appear, making chips from right of the green a touchy proposition at best. Like most par-5s, this hole gives up its share of birdies; and like the second hole, its share of round-busting disasters, too.

## No. 7 – Par 3
(185/175/170/165)

The strongest par-3 on the course features one of the toughest greens to putt. Bunkers guard both sides of the green, with some room available beyond the left bunker. Shots that land just short and right of the putting surface often bounce onto the green.

The middle of the green is never a bad place to be here, but there are putts you'd rather not leave yourself. For example, if the pin is back center or back left, avoid the right half of the green at all costs. The slope back there is severe toward the left, making three putts a distinct probability.

Pin positions in the front right quarter of the green feature a fairly severe slope toward the front center. You actually may be better off just short of the green than beyond the flag. The most difficult position to get close to with the tee shot is back right, where a plateau falls away toward the back of the green. Par on this hole is always a good score.

## No. 8 – Par 4
(393/381/368/365)

The only dead-straight hole on the course often plays into the wind and features a tricky green to hit. Framing bunkers on either side of the fairway are more of an issue for longer hitters. The right-side bunker is nearer the tee and can be carried when conditions are right.

The fairway slopes to the right, kicking shots hit down the right-center of the fairway toward that right bunker. Anything right of the bunker is blocked by trees and low-hanging branches, and even a punch out from there is no easy task.

The left side is the preferred line because of the angle of the green and the presence of a large bunker on the right. The green is deeper on the right side and slopes away from the bunker, especially in the front half of the green. The back of the green slopes significantly toward the front, making chips from over the green virtually impossible to get close to back pins.

## No. 9 – Par 4
(444/426/401)

For my money, this is the toughest hole on the course. A par-4½ for most players and an outright par-5 for higher handicappers, it's not unheard of for par to walk away with a skin here in larger group events. Even the scratch guys breathe a sigh of relief after marking 4 on their card.

Depending on conditions, the downhill tee shot on this dogleg-left hole can require anything from a driver – often requiring more distance than some players can generate – down to 3-wood or less. Find the flat landing area from 190 to 150 yards from the green, and you improve your chances for a good score significantly.

However, hitting that safe zone is easier said than done. Anything left is blocked or goes down into a lower area that also brings a hazard into play. Play too safely down the right side and you bring ball-gobbling cedar trees and thick bushes into play, along with the probability of a difficult, downhill lie and a longer second shot.

In order to get into the 160-yard range, you need to cut the corner of the dogleg or play a right-to-left shot that follows the contour of the hole and the hill. Too far left or not far enough and you're stuck behind the trees on the corner. Too far right and you can go through the fairway and bring trees into play. It's a fine line between perfection and trouble.

As if that's not enough, Trout Creek makes its way across the fairway about 120 yards from the green. This poses no problem if you've negotiated your tee shot successfully, but short hitters or anyone in the woods will need to seriously consider laying up and playing the hole as a three-shot par-5.

From the creek, it's all uphill to a wide green that slopes toward the front left. The hill is steep enough that it requires virtually all carry to get to the green. Be careful when putting downhill, because it's common to run well past the hole when the greens are at their summer speeds. The back portions of the green are the most difficult, but there is no such thing as an easy putt on the ninth hole.

## No. 10 – Par 5
(514/501/453/407)

Despite its modest length for a par-5, the tenth requires considerable length off the tee to realistically get near the green in two. That's because the hill on the opposite side of Trout Creek's valley acts like a wall. Carry that hill and you enjoy a normal rollout; hit into the hill and your drive comes to a screeching halt.

The popular line off the tee is along the edge of the rough on the right side, because the fairway doglegs right at this point and there is a little room for error in the rough. The risk/reward factor comes in the form of trees and bushes on that side that separate the tenth fairway from the ninth.

It's common to hear players urging tee shots heading too far right to "get more right!" and all the way through to the ninth fairway. From there, the play is up the ninth fairway, setting up a third shot over the trees near the ninth tee and back to the tenth green. Nothing is more irritating to your opponent than making par from the wrong fairway (so I hear).

For most players, the second shot comes from an uphill lie to a blind fairway. The line is just right of the big willow tree you can see left of the fairway, about 80 yards short of the green. A sand trap about 30 yards short of the green defines an opening to the left portion of the green. Another bunker left of the green comes into play particularly when attempting a punch shot under the low-hanging branches of the willow tree.

The green slopes severely toward the right front, and any downhill putt is extremely fast.

## No. 11 – Par 4
(444/429/404/401)

This is the beginning of Brown County's version of Amen Corner. Make it through the next three beautiful holes cleanly and chances are good you'll have a successful back nine. The eleventh ranks as the most difficult handicap hole on the inward nine.

This strong par-4 requires good length off the tee to gain an unobstructed view of the green around the dogleg right. Beware of trying to cut too much off the dogleg, as the trees extend farther down the fairway than it looks from the tee. For those with good length, the popular target is down the right rough line, just right of the red maple tree through the opposite end of the fairway.

Balls bounce to the right down that side, which can bring overhanging branches about 130 yards from the green into play. They can force a significant left-to-right shape or a punch shot for your approach. The trees down the right side line a ravine that plays as a lateral hazard. Find that hazard and you'll have a drop with no shot at the green and almost automatic double bogey.

The downhill approach is one of the prettier views on the course, especially in the fall. Traps guard the large green around the left side and behind. The only safe miss here is short. Do not, under any circumstances, short-side yourself. The bowl-contoured green slopes toward the middle and front, sending chips speeding past the hole from most angles. Back pin positions become increasingly brutal the farther right and back they go.

## No. 12 – Par 4
(399/373/325/320)

A scenic bend in Duck Creek flows in front of the blue and white tees, creating more of a visual effect than a practical hazard. However, the creek continues up the right side and does catch its share of sliced tee shots. Longer hitters may want to consider something less than a driver here since the 150-yard mark, at which point the fairway narrows and turns slightly right, is a good position.

The fairway seems to set up for a slight left-to-right shot off the tee, but the opposite is actually the safer play. Thick woods down the right side are not the place to be. It's even possible to be in the fairway down the right side and still have branches obstructing your desired flight path.

Instead, the safer play is down the more open left side, where there is room even in the rough to play a normal second shot as long as you don't run all the way through to the trees. The fairway is flat all the way to the green, making run-up shots possible.

Avoid the bunkers right of the green, since the putting surface runs away from that position. The left portion of the green is shallow and easy to hit through. However, chipping from the left side still is preferable to anything long or right, and the left side absolutely is the place to be when the pin is in the back-left or back-center portions of the green.

## No. 13 – Par 4
(349/334/290/288)

What a fun hole this is. Not long, but strategic, pretty and potentially lethal. It's the perfect ending to a great three-hole stretch of par-4s.

This dogleg-left beauty features a variety of hazards just waiting to crush your spirit. Duck Creek passes silently behind a line of trees down the right side of the fairway; the first of three ponds sits beyond a line of trees down the left; a second pond fronts the green and wraps around the right side; and a sand trap that sits out of sight left of the green protects balls from bouncing into a third pond beyond that.

*The well-guarded green at the par-4 thirteenth at Brown County
(Photo Mike Dauplaise)*

If you remember the tip from earlier, you took note of the pin position on this green as you walked up the hill to your tee shot on the fifth hole. Here's why you did that: If the pin is in the left half of the thirteenth green – especially toward the back – you'll want to be as far down the fairway as possible to create the best angle of attack for your approach.

Choose a club off the tee that will get you to about 100 yards from the green. That spot is near the end of the fairway before it turns left toward the green. The green slopes hard inward from the left, so hitting your approach from a position as far down the fairway as possible will allow you to land into that slope rather than on a downslope.

Do not try to cut the dogleg from the tee, because the pond that fronts the green comes into play just beyond the first pond on the left. A narrow isthmus divides the two ponds, and it's not worth the risk to sneak a drive into that area. You only have a short iron in from the middle of the fairway anyway.

The front of the green is a false front. In fact, for pin positions near the point of no return, you're almost better off chipping up the hill than putting from behind the hole. You might end up in the front fringe anyway after your first putt. When the greens are fast, this hole is truly diabolical.

**No. 14 – Par 5**
(562/484/474/469)

As the listed yardages imply, there is a big difference if playing the blue tees here. There are some players who can get home in two from the white tees, but few who can do it from the blues.

The preferred target is along the right rough line at the top of a plateau. This line accounts for the gentle dogleg-left shape of the fairway beyond, as well as the left slope of the hill, which increasingly moves left on the backside of the plateau. Anything hit long enough to clear the crest of the hill must be on that line to have any chance of staying in the fairway.

Shots hit too far to the right risk catching a natural area or being blocked by trees there, while anything hit down the middle will run left into the rough and take away the option of an aggressive second shot. If your group has anyone waiting for the green to clear before hitting their second shot, it's a good idea to position someone back on the plateau so the group behind doesn't hit into you.

Up at the green, there is an opening between a front-left bunker and another on the right. The contour off the right bunker helps kick balls toward the center of the green. For that reason, the best position to approach any right-side pin is the left side of the fairway. There is more green behind the front left bunker than you can see from the fairway, but it isn't as deep as the right side of the green and slopes away from the fairway.

It doesn't take overly aggressive play to have a good shot at birdie on the fourteenth, which is a welcome respite after the challenges of the previous three holes.

*Bunkers guard the undulating green on the par-3 fifteenth at Brown County (Mike Dauplaise photo)*

## No. 15 – Par 3
(154/145/141/137)

The final hole in the Duck Creek valley uses the severe contours of this green as its primary defense. The greens renovation project included arguably more dramatic changes to this bowl-contoured putting surface than any other. Additional shelves provide new pin placements and have changed the way players allow for rollouts.

Times were when any approach shot into the opening on the left half of the green would automatically feed down to the low area of the bowl. That's not necessarily the case anymore with the addition of a shelf halfway down the slope. Since leaving yourself a downhill putt from the wrong shelf is almost automatic three-putt territory, it's even more important to challenge the bunker short and right of the green to leave a more manageable first putt.

There are two bunkers left of the green that players must avoid at all costs. It's all downhill from there, making it virtually impossible to save par for any pin position not in the bottom of the bowl. There is more green available behind the right bunker than is visible from the tee, and that area features its own mini-bowl contour.

Par is common here, but there are oh, so many ways to pile up strokes around this green.

## No. 16 – Par 4
(397/382/375/370)

Climb the steep hill adjacent to the fifteenth green and catch your breath before tackling the home stretch. The sixteenth is a fairly straightforward par-4 that encourages a right-to-left shot shape to follow the gentle dogleg.

A framing bunker left of the landing area encourages shots to the right side, which in many cases provides a better angle into the green anyway. Trees line both sides of the hole, but there is plenty of space in the rough prior to reaching any trouble.

Bunkers positioned short left and right of the wide green come into play. Short-side misses produce extremely difficult par saves as the green runs away from either angle. The green is open in front for the downhill approach, allowing easy run-on access. In fact, landing short left and allowing the ball to release is an effective strategy for front pin positions.

The green generally slopes toward the middle and front center, meaning your best angles of attack come from the opposite sides of the fairway: left side for right pins and right side for left pins.

## No. 17 – Par 3
(177/158/111/107)

The final par-3 is the most picturesque, playing downhill over a retention pond and Trout Creek to a round green that slopes right to left. There is plenty of room beyond the hazard to bounce shots onto the green, and the mowed area in front also offers the easiest chipping.

Two bunkers right of the green are death because the green slopes severely away from that angle. Play toward the middle of the green for any pin positions on the right side, and favor the left side for back-center pin positions. Good luck two-putting if you leave yourself a downhill or sidehill putt in those areas of the green.

## No. 18 – Par 4
(397/385/355/353)

This dogleg-right finisher plays longer than listed thanks to an uphill tee shot that heads into the prevailing wind. In fact, many players don't have enough length off the tee to get past the huge oaks and other tall timbers that comprise the dogleg, forcing a cut shot around the corner or a punch through an alley in the woods.

For the bigger hitters, it is possible to land on top of the plateau and drive through the fairway, bringing a large tree about 80 yards from the green on the left side into play. Too far left or long also introduces jail in the form of "the well," an area down an embankment that's home to the maintenance buildings. You can find your ball down there, but trees and bushes make executing even a punch shot back to safety no sure bet.

Do not try going over the trees on the corner, even if you think you have the length (you probably don't). The distance needed to carry the tall trees makes it impossible to hold the fairway beyond without getting into trouble on the opposite side. Just take a shorter club off the tee if you have to, and play to the safe area about 150 yards from the green.

If you're feeling aggressive, go ahead and try to skirt the edge of the dogleg and bounce through to about 130 yards. It's not unheard of for misses right of that to find the alley and still make it through the woods to the fairway. It's a risk/reward situation that you'll need to assess for yourself.

If you take that route and don't quite make it far enough into the fairway, you'll find yourself behind an additional pair of oaks that hangs over the right side of the fairway about 80 yards from the green.

The green is slightly elevated and open in front, with bunkers on both sides that must be avoided if a short-side situation exists. The bowl-contoured green is especially steep toward the back, making it imperative to putt from below the hole.

**Summary**

There's a reason Brown County long held a place among the top municipal courses in the country, and the new greens have restored it to its former glory. While not on par with the elite courses an hour to the south, it doesn't pretend to be. The County is a much more affordable option, certainly more user-friendly for all ability levels, and definitely worth a visit.

# Acknowledgements

One does not embark on a tour of some of the country's most spectacular golf courses without a little trepidation about potential cost. After all, I'm just a writer guy with predictably limited funds.

That's why my first thanks go to the course owners and managers who generously allowed me to play their magnificent properties in the name of "research." Earlier in my career, I wrote a true crime book that was an emotional and time-consuming challenge from a research perspective. Putting together golf destination guides like this is a tad more enjoyable, and cooperation from the courses certainly helps in that regard.

The courses also were very generous with photos when available. A golf destination guide needs to have some eye candy, and there's no question these properties have that in spades. The Kohler Communications team, in particular, gave this project a much-needed visual boost when they gave me access to their library of phenomenal images and a treasure trove of background information.

I also want to thank my proofreaders for making sure my descriptions were accurate and easy to follow. My longtime golf partner, Jeff Wickwire, would whip through chapters and get back to me with feedback often within a couple of hours; and Charlie Spain, who caddied for me at the Irish Course recently and at the Straits Course more than a decade earlier, gave my Kohler chapters a first read before I sent them off to the Communications team for a final check.

Sincere thanks go to my awesome wife, Bonnie Groessl. Bonnie and I are partners on an entrepreneurial journey that requires us to be self-motivated and self-starting. She is an angel for her patience in allowing me to pursue my golf passion when there are always more important things I could be doing.

And finally, I want to thank you for taking the time to read my book. I hope my efforts help you enjoy these great golf courses and leave you with lasting memories. If you would be so kind as to recommend this book on social media and post a review on Amazon, I would be most appreciative.

Mike

*Golf in Eastern Wisconsin*

*The author at the Irish Course with his favorite Whistling Straits caddie, Charlie Spain.*

# About the Author

Mike Dauplaise is a professional writer based in Green Bay, Wisconsin. He is a lifelong golf nut who played collegiately at St. Norbert College in De Pere, Wis., and has been writing about golf for more than thirty years. A three-time qualifier for the Wisconsin State Amateur, Mike carries a handicap in the mid-single digits.

Mike began his writing career as a newspaper reporter and copy editor for the *Green Bay Press-Gazette*, *Wausau (Wis.) Daily Herald* and *Green Bay News-Chronicle*. He transitioned into corporate communications and eventually the world of the self-employed. In addition to writing for business and institutional clients, he has authored, co-authored or ghost-authored five books and edited more than a dozen others.

Mike's golf articles have appeared in a variety of magazines, including *Wisconsin Golf*, *Par Excellence* and *Great Lakes Golf*.

You can see more of Mike's writing work on Amazon, http://www.mikedauplaise.com and at http://primegolfdestinations.com.

*Golf in Eastern Wisconsin*

www.ingramcontent.com/pod-product-compliance
Lightning Source LLC
Chambersburg PA
CBHW042233090526

44588CB00001B/1